Table of Contents

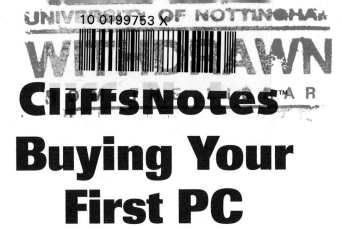

CliffsNotes™

Buying Your First PC

PCs in the
online   at

About the Author

Joe Kraynak has taught hundreds of thousands of new PC users how to make the most of their PCs with his easy-to-read books, including *The Complete Idiot's Guide to PCs, Big Basics Book of Windows 98,* and *Sams Teach Yourself Notebook Basics in Ten Minutes.*

Publisher's Acknowledgments

Editorial

Project Editor: Paul Levesque
Acquisitions Editor: Joyce Pepple
Copy Editor: Bill Barton
Technical Editor: Lee Musick

Production

Indexer: York Production Services, Inc.
Proofreader: York Production Services, Inc.
IDG Books Indianapolis Production Department

CliffsNotes™ Buying Your First PC

Published by
IDG Books Worldwide, Inc.
An International Data Group Company
919 E. Hillsdale Blvd.
Suite 400
Foster City, CA 94404
www.idgbooks.com (IDG Books Worldwide Web site)
www.cliffsnotes.com (CliffsNotes Web site)

Library of Congress Catalog Card No.: 99-66716
ISBN: 0-7645-8521-5
Printed in the United States of America
10 9 8 7 6 5 4 3 2 1
10/QS/RS/ZZ/IN

100199753 X

Distributed in the United States by IDG Books Worldwide, Inc.
Distributed by CDG Books Canada Inc. for Canada; by Transworld Publishers Limited in the United Kingdom; by IDG Norge Books for Norway; by IDG Sweden Books for Sweden; by IDG Books Australia Publishing Corporation Pty. Ltd. for Australia and New Zealand; by TransQuest Publishers Pte Ltd. for Singapore, Malaysia, Thailand, Indonesia, and Hong Kong; by Gotop Information Inc. for Taiwan; by ICG Muse, Inc. for Japan; by Intersoft for South Africa; by Eyrolles for France; by International Thomson Publishing for Germany, Austria and Switzerland; by Distribuidora Cuspide for Argentina; by LR International for Brazil; by Galileo Libros for Chile; by Ediciones ZETA S.C.R. Ltda. for Peru; by WS Computer Publishing Corporation, Inc., for the Philippines; by Contemporanea de Ediciones for Venezuela; by Express Computer Distributors for the Caribbean and West Indies; by Micronesia Media Distributor, Inc. for Micronesia; by Chips Computadoras S.A. de C.V. for Mexico; by Editorial Norma de Panama S.A. for Panama; by American Bookshops for Finland.
For general information on IDG Books Worldwide's books in the U.S., please call our Consumer Customer Service department at **800-762-2974.** For reseller information, including discounts and premium sales, please call our Reseller Customer Service department at **800-434-3422.**
For information on where to purchase IDG Books Worldwide's books outside the U.S., please contact our International Sales department at 317-596-5530 or fax **317-596-5692.**
For consumer information on foreign language translations, please contact our Customer Service department at **1-800-434-3422,** fax **317-596-5692,** or e-mail rights@idgbooks.com.
For information on licensing foreign or domestic rights, please phone **+1-650-655-3109.**
For sales inquiries and special prices for bulk quantities, please contact our Sales department at 650-655-3200 or write to the address above.
For information on using IDG Books Worldwide's books in the classroom or for ordering examination copies, please contact our Educational Sales department at **800-434-2086** or fax **317-596-5499.**
For press review copies, author interviews, or other publicity information, please contact our Public Relations department at **650-655-3000** or fax **650-655-3299.**
For authorization to photocopy items for corporate, personal, or educational use, please contact Copyright Clearance Center, 222 Rosewood Drive, Danvers, MA 01923, or fax **978-750-4470.**

INTRODUCTION

With PC prices in a continuous free-fall, even the most technically challenged are flocking to the computer stores to buy their first PC. But where do you start? How do you avoid getting stuck by the sticker price? Who can you trust?

Welcome to CliffsNotes *Buying Your First PC*. In this book, I don't tell you how to buy the biggest, fastest supercomputer on the market. And because I'm not a salesperson, I don't hype cutting edge technology. In plain and simple terms, I show you how to track down the right PC for your needs and budget.

Why Do You Need This Book?

Can you answer yes to any of these questions?

- Do you need to purchase a good PC fast?
- Don't have time to read 500 pages on the inner workings of PC components?
- Are you afraid that a dealer will sell you more PC than you need?
- Are you concerned that the PC you buy today will be obsolete tomorrow?
- Do PC terms like Pentium, Celeron, AGP, and DMA make your eyes glassy?

If so, then CliffsNotes *Buying Your First PC* is for you!

How to Use This Book

You can read this book straight through or just look for the information you need. You can find information on a particular topic in a number of ways: You can search the index in the back of the book, locate your topic in the Table of Contents, or read the In This Chapter list in each chapter. To reinforce your learning, check out the Review and the Resource Center at the back of the book. To help you find important information in the book, look for the following icons in the text:

This icon points out something worth keeping in mind.

This icon clues you in to helpful hints and advice.

This icon alerts you to something dangerous or to avoid.

Don't Miss Our Web Site

Keep up with the exciting world of personal computers by visiting the CliffsNotes Web site at www.cliffs-notes.com. Here's what you find:

■ Interactive tools that are fun and informative.

■ Links to interesting Web sites.

■ Additional resources to help you continue your learning.

At www.cliffsnotes.com, you can even register for CliffsNotes Daily, a free daily newsletter on a variety of topics that we deliver right to your e-mail inbox each business day.

If you haven't yet discovered the Internet and are wondering how to get online, pick up CliffsNotes *Getting On the Internet*, new from CliffsNotes. You'll learn just what you need to make your online connection quickly and easily. See you at www.cliffsnotes.com!

CHAPTER 1

ASSESSING YOUR COMPUTING NEEDS

IN THIS CHAPTER

- Taking stock of your business computing needs
- Gathering input from family members
- Listing the programs you want to run
- Determining PC requirements for running programs

When you shop for any big-ticket item — a car, refrigerator, or TV set — you need to consider not only the quality of the machine but also how you plan to use it. If you have three kids to taxi around, you may decide that that Porsche Boxster you've been drooling over isn't the most practical vehicle for your situation.

The same is true when you shop for a PC. If you're buying a PC so that you can send e-mail, manage your personal finances, and check out the Internet, you don't need a humongous monitor and cool stereo speakers. A basic system with a fast modem for connecting to the Internet will suit your needs. Now if you're buying a PC for your discerning family (and you don't want your kid to think you passed up the Nikes for a pair of Keds), a humongous monitor and cool stereo speakers may very well be essential.

Keeping this in mind, follow the three-step process detailed in this chapter to assess your computing needs before you even glance at a PC ad:

1. Make a list of what you want to do with the PC. Don't forget that if you're planning to use your PC mainly for business purposes, your needs are different than if you plan on letting your new PC be the family computer. Tables 1-1 and 1-2 can help you here.

2. Determine which programs you need to accomplish each task. Be generous. Include those programs you may conceivably use farther down the road. You want to plan some extra room for growth. Again, Tables 1-1 and 1-2 can show you how it's done.

3. Determine the PC requirements for running the programs. I show you how to do this in the section "Shopping Backwards: Software First," later in this chapter.

Sizing Up Your Business Needs

Buying a PC for business purposes makes perfect sense. After all, PCs started out as business machines — tools that made it easier to type letters, process orders, track payroll and inventory, and manage records. Their role in business hasn't diminished. PCs are still useful for typing documents, designing and printing publications, and managing financial data. In fact, the role of PCs in business has grown. You can now use a PC to send and receive faxes, communicate via e-mail, place your business on the World Wide Web, video conference, and waste loads of time playing Solitaire.

Now, don't run out and purchase the first PC that's advertised as a "Business PC." Business PCs vary as widely as different businesses. If your job consists of some light typing, a basic PC system can serve you well. On the other hand, if you're planning on starting your own graphic design company, where you hope to use bunches of memory-hungry computer drawing programs, you need a powerful PC with gobs of memory and a big monitor. (Don't let all this talk about *memory* scare you. You get the lowdown on memory and other computer specifications in Chapters 4 and 7.)

If you're buying a PC to bring a little work home on the weekends, purchase a PC that's comparable to the one you use in your office. If your office PC can run circles around your home PC, you'll hate working on your home PC.

To determine your business computing needs, write down a list of what you plan on doing with your PC. Use Table 1-1 as a model. Don't forget that you're not buying a computer to have something pretty sitting on your desk; you're buying it to help you do the work you do. And the different kinds of work you do determines what kind of PC you end up buying. So, get started on that list and make it as complete as possible.

Table 1-1:   Your Business Computing Needs

If You Want to . . .	*You Need the Following Computer Program Type . . .*
Type	Word processor, such as Microsoft Word or WordPerfect
Paint/draw	Graphics, such as CorelDRAW or Adobe Photoshop
Create ads and other publications	Desktop publishing, such as Microsoft Publisher or PageMaker
Manage payroll and inventory	Accounting, such as QuickBooks or Peachtree
Calculate and analyze financial data	Spreadsheet, such as Excel or Lotus 1-2-3
Manage data/records	Database, such as Access or Paradox
Plan and bill projects	Project manager, such as Microsoft Project or Milestones Etc.

(continued)

Table 1-1:   Your Business Computing Needs
(continued)

If You Want to . . .	You Need the Following Computer Program Type . . .
Plan and pay taxes	Tax, such as TurboTax or Kiplinger TaxCut
Manage schedules	Personal information manager, such as Outlook or Organizer
Keep track of contacts	Contact manager, such as ACT! or GoldMine
Create presentations	Business presentation, such as PowerPoint or Harvard Graphics
Create Web pages	Web page editor, such as FrontPage or Web Studio
Send and receive e-mail	Email, such as Outlook Express or Eudora

Ask your colleagues and business associates about the software and PCs they use. They can give advice that stems from practical experience, such as creating reports, tracking payroll, and buying from a dealer that offers reliable service.

Considering Your Family's Needs

Shopping for a family PC is almost as tough as deciding where to eat out on soccer night — you must consider the needs and desires of all family members (even if you choose to ignore them). You may want to use the PC to print custom greeting cards and banners, while your spouse wants to track investments and your kid wants to blast aliens and do a little creative plagiarizing for school reports.

Instead of sitting down on your own and making a list (like the one you used to assess your business needs), call a family meeting and make a list together. Use Table 1-2 as a model. Make sure that all family members make their wishes known.

(It saves pain and heartache later.) And feel free to add to the list yourself.

Table 1-2: Your Home Computer Needs

If a Family Member Wants to . . .	You Need to Get . . .
Type letters	A word processing program or a suite, such as Home Essentials or Office
Print a resume	A word processing program or a suite, such as Home Essentials or Office
Find a job	A modem and Internet or online service
Research topics	CD-ROM reference titles, such as Encarta or Home Medical Advisor
Research topics on the Internet	A modem and Internet or online service
Reinforce school lessons	Educational software, such as Reader Rabbit or MathBlaster
Play games	Games, such as Myth or NFL Blitz, a fast PC with gobs of memory, 3D audio, a 19-inch monitor, a graphics adapter with 4 megabytes RAM, and a joystick
Make greeting cards	Desktop publishing program, such as Print Shop or Microsoft Publisher
Print signs and banners	Desktop publishing program, such as Print Shop or Microsoft Publisher
Manage a checkbook	Personal finance program, such as Quicken or Microsoft Money
Send e-mail	E-mail program, such as Outlook Express or Eudora
Get music clips from the Web	A modem, online service, stereo sound card, and speakers

(continued)

Table 1-2:   Your Home Computer Needs
**   (continued)**

If a Family Member Wants to . . .	You Need to Get . . .
Read current news clips	A modem and Internet or online service
Plan a vacation	A modem and Internet or online service
Shop	A modem and Internet or online service
Make a cool Web site	A modem and Internet or online service

Most family PCs come with basic software installed. Such offerings typically include a word processor, spreadsheet, address book, e-mail program, and software for finding and connecting to an online service (and the Internet).

Shopping Backwards: Software First

One of the biggest mistakes people make when selecting their first PC is to overlook the software (programs) and focus entirely on the hardware (the PC itself). Admittedly, the PC is essential, but it's the programs that do all the cool stuff. The PC just does what the programs tell it to do — assuming, of course, that the PC has what it takes to do the job.

By neglecting software issues, you risk facing some major headaches soon after you get your PC home. You'll run out and buy the game you always wanted to play only to learn that your PC doesn't have the right audio card, enough memory, or that crucial joystick you need to fly your virtual F-111.

To avoid these costly, frustrating mistakes, shop for software first.

Shopping for software

You have your lists detailing what you and your family members want to do with the PC. Perhaps you even have a general idea of the types of programs you want to run. Maybe a colleague suggested that you use Microsoft Word for word processing, or your daughter has been playing with Reader Rabbit at her friend's house, or you've seen commercials or ads for programs you want to check out.

Write down the name of each program you want to investigate and make sure you have at least one program listed for each task you want your PC to perform. (Look at the lists you created earlier.) After you have your task list in hand, take the following steps to determine which programs you want to use:

1. Ask your friends, relatives, and colleagues for recommendations.

2. Ask your kids' teachers for a list of games and educational programs they use in the classroom.

3. Visit a local PC users group and ask for recommendations. (Check your local computer stores for information about users groups.)

4. Read software reviews in computer magazines or on the Internet.

5. Take a drive to your local computer store and ask the salesperson whether you can try out the programs on your list. (If you're buying a family PC, take your family along.)

The best time to join a PC users group is *before* you purchase a PC. Users groups can steer you clear of irresponsible local dealers, help you find great deals, and recommend or even offer classes to teach you how to use your PC.

Calculating the hardware requirements

No, your job's not over, yet. Make some copies of the handy-dandy Program Requirements Form (Figure 1-1), and with your blank forms in hand, go back to the computer store and start researching the minimum hardware requirements for the software you're interested in. (Not too difficult a task, since every software program should have a list of the minimum requirements for running the program somewhere on the package.) Enter all the pertinent information for each software program on a separate form. You'll find information about the type of processor required, the minimum amount of RAM needed, the necessary operating system (for example, Windows 98), the amount of disk space required, and whether you'll need any special hardware (such as a joystick or modem). Don't worry if you encounter terms or specifications you don't understand; I tell you about these terms (and about reading ads) in Chapter 4.

Figure 1-1: The program requirements form.

Program Name:

Price:

Operating System:

Processor:

Memory Required:

Memory Recommended:

Hard Drive Space:

CD-ROM Drive Speed:

Display/Video/Graphics:

Audio/Sound board:

Printer type:

Additional requirements:

After you complete the forms, flip through the stack and consolidate the information on a single copy of the Program Requirements Form. Take the following steps to consolidate the information:

1. Write down the most powerful processor required. For example, if one package requires a 486 processor and another requires a Pentium, write down Pentium. Here's a list of processors ranked from most to least powerful:

> Intel Pentium Xeon (mostly for network servers)
> Intel Pentium III or AMD-K6III (for power users)
> Cyrix MII (for bargain hunters)
> Intel Pentium II
> Intel Celeron or AMD-K6II (for casual users)
> Intel Pentium Pro
> Intel Pentium with MMX (for multimedia)
> Intel 486 (obsolete)

Processor speeds can be deceiving. A 200 MHz Pentium III processor is faster than a 300 MHz Celeron processor. Don't worry about speeds for now; I tell you more about processor speeds in Chapter 4.

2. Write down the largest amount of RAM (random access memory) required to run any one of the programs.

3. Add up the hard drive (disk space) requirements from each of the software programs to determine the minimum amount of disk space you need to run all programs. Each 1000 megabytes (MB) roughly equals one gigabyte (GB). Multiply this sum by 5 (so that you'll have room for additional programs and the files you create) and write down the result.

4. Write down the fastest CD-ROM drive required by any one of the programs.

5. Record the operating system required (for example, Windows 95 or Windows NT).

6. Write down any special video requirements. In most cases, you'll purchase an SVGA monitor (short for *Super Video Graphics Array*), but the program may require a special graphics adapter (or display card) that has additional memory.

7. Record the audio requirements — for example, Sound-Blaster or AdLib.

8. Write down any additional hardware or software — such as a modem, joystick, MIDI port (for musical input), or microphone — that's required to run or use a program.

When you're done with the consolidated version of your program requirements form, you have a pretty good idea of the *least* you should look for in a PC. The following sections explain some additional issues to consider.

Be sure to check the required operating system (the program that enables your PC to run all other programs). Common operating systems include Windows 98, Windows 95, Windows NT, Windows 2000, and Mac/OS.

Additional Computing Issues

At first, you may think that you and your family will use the PC primarily to create and print documents and play a few games. However, as you use the PC, you begin to realize that you can tap more resources and perform tasks you never imagined. By looking ahead, you can ensure that your family PC is equipped to handle the possibilities. The following sections help you peer into the future.

E-mail and the Web

Whether you plan on using your PC for business, pleasure, or education, you eventually want to connect to the Internet to exchange e-mail messages, explore Web pages, shop, and grab free stuff. In short, don't even consider purchasing a family PC without a modem.

What kind of modem should you get? For standard phone line connections, purchase a 56 Kbps modem. (*Kbps*, or kilobytes per second, represents the speed of the modem.) Faster options are available, depending on what the cable and phone companies in your area support. I tell you more about modems in Chapters 2 and 3, which help you when you actually start shopping.

Not all standard phone lines support 56 Kbps connections. In some areas, the speed is limited to 33.6 Kbps or (gasp!) 28.8 Kbps. Check with your phone company.

Games, graphics, and music

For the fun-loving, media-hungry members of your family (which probably includes you), a PC with powerful audio and video capabilities is essential. Computer games require a display card and monitor that can quickly generate images and handle animations. Likewise, computer graphics and music clips require a powerful processor (brain cell) and high-quality video and audio devices.

At this point, I'm not going to list the PC components required to play media files (audio and video clips, complex graphics, and animations). Just keep in mind that you need to raise your expectations a bit (and dig a little deeper into your bank account) if you're looking for a PC that doubles as an entertainment center and game machine. In Chapters 2 and 3, I talk about specific requirements.

If your kid wants a game machine, buy a Sony Playstation or Nintendo 64 for a couple of hundred bucks. You'll save enough money on your PC to pay for the game machine, and you won't have to fight your kid for time on the PC.

TV and other media

People don't generally purchase a PC to watch TV on it, but if you're planning on purchasing a small TV for your den and you have no idea of where you're going to place it, consider purchasing a PC with a TV tuner card.

A TV tuner card enables you to connect your PC with cable TV, an antenna, or a VCR so that you can use it to watch TV and videos. Windows 98 includes a program called Web TV, which (with the help of a modem) can help you view current TV listings and tune into your favorite shows.

You can purchase TV tuner cards separately or buy an all-in-one display card that functions as a video adapter (for connecting the monitor) and a TV tuner. The advantage of an all-in-one card is that it occupies only one expansion slot inside your PC and leaves room for installing additional hardware later.

Choosing a PC for road trips

Everyone *wants* a notebook (laptop) PC. You can plug it into an outlet in any room in the house, tote it into your next job interview, and even stuff it in an airplane's carryon luggage compartment. The question is: Do you want to pay double the price for portability? That's about how much extra a notebook PC costs over a comparably equipped desktop model.

Notebook computers also have several other disadvantages when compared to desktop PCs:

- The keyboard is cramped.

- The screen is tiny, even on *big-screen* notebooks.

- The speakers and microphone are anemic.

- Touchpads and other built-in pointing devices are no match for a mouse.

- Upgrading is typically expensive and complicated.

- It's hot. The processor, which puts out a lot of heat, typically sits right under the palm of your hand.

- It's easy to steal (not that I've ever stolen one).

I recommend purchasing a desktop PC first, but if you need to take your computing show on the road, a notebook or other lightweight device (such as a handheld PC) is your only choice.

When shopping for a notebook PC, follow the same rule for determining the hardware requirements: software first.

Although you should always try a PC before buying it, the try-before-you-buy rule is especially important for notebook PCs. Keyboards, displays, and pointing devices vary widely among notebooks; make sure that you're comfortable using the features of any notebook you're considering.

CHAPTER 2
PICKING A PRICE RANGE

IN THIS CHAPTER

- Finding a "free" PC
- Checking out different price ranges
- Matching a PC to your needs and budget
- Finding a general PC package that's right for you

Shopping for a PC is kind of like shopping for a VCR player. At first, you just want the thing to play tapes. After you shop around a little while, you find out that you can get a player with input jacks for your camcorder, output jacks for speakers, and fancy programming controls for taping your favorite shows. You end up walking out of the store with a machine that does a lot more than just play tapes and costs a bit more than you had planned on spending.

Most PC dealers (retail or mail order) feature preconfigured PCs (package deals) put together to serve the needs of a particular customer type: bargain hunter, casual user, family user, or business user. A basic family PC, for example, typically comes with a Celeron processor (a step down from a Pentium II), 32 megabytes of RAM (just enough to get by), a 15-inch monitor, a five to six gigabyte hard drive (sufficient storage for most users), a CD-ROM drive, a stereo sound card and speakers, a modem, and a suite of home-based software, all for around a thousand bucks.

You can then choose to soup up the basic system by choosing a more powerful processor, additional RAM, a larger monitor, and so on.

Before you start considering your options, you want to check out some of the package deals available and pick a price range that's pretty close to what you're willing to spend. The sections in this chapter show you how much PC you can expect to get by shopping in various price ranges.

What Can I Get for Free?

You can get a lot of PC for free, assuming that you agree to the conditions of the "gift" and that the giver chooses you as one of the lucky recipients. A company by the name of Free-PC Network gives away pretty good entry-level PCs to selected applicants. At the time of this writing, Free-PC Network is handing out PCs that meet the specifications in Table 2-1. Figure 2-1 shows the PC in action, but Free-PC is constantly trying to obtain more powerful PCs, so the PC you get may differ.

Table 2-1: Free-PC Specifications

Component/Software	Specification/Offering
Processor	Celeron 300 MHz (Megahertz, the speed at which the processor "thinks")
Memory	32MB RAM
Hard drive	4GB
Modem	56 Kbps (Kilobytes per second, the speed of the modem)
Removable storage	Floppy drive, 24X CD-ROM drive (24X refers to the CD-ROM drive speed; I recommend 32X or faster)

(continued)

Table 2-1:   Free-PC Specifications *(continued)*

Component/Software	*Specification/Offering*
Monitor	SVGA 15-inch color (SVGA, short for Super Video Graphics Array, is standard for high-quality monitors)
Input devices	Keyboard, mouse
Audio	Sound card and speakers
Operating system	Windows 98
E-mail	Outlook
Software	Basic word processor, if any software is included
Web browser	Internet Explorer 4.0

Figure 2-1:   A free PC is a nice, basic machine, assuming that you don't mind a little advertising. (Photo courtesy of Free-PC, Inc.)

So what's the catch? Free-PC sets up an innovative trade between prospective PC users and advertisers: You get a PC, *for free*, and in return, you must supply Free-PC with marketing data that it can pass along to its partners. In addition, you must agree to display targeted advertisements around the border of your monitor. You still have enough room to work on documents and use your other programs, but on a 15-inch monitor, you may feel a little cramped.

If you're a new PC user who doesn't have a lot of money to plop down on a top-of the line PC, however, a free PC — even with the constant on-screen advertising — offers an affordable solution for getting started and connecting to the Internet. (If you have access to the Internet, you can check out Free-PC Network at `www.free-pc.com`.)

Many merchants offer free or heavily discounted PCs with the purchase of a subscription to an online service (typically at a cost of $500-$700). The Better Business Bureau has been swamped with complaints about free PC deals, so be careful out there.

$500 or Less

The price to beat in the PC market is $500. By bringing the cost of a PC in line with that of a camcorder or a TV set, manufacturers and dealers hope to tap into the home market in a big way. Face it — five hundred bucks for a PC is a very attractive deal.

If you see a PC for $500 or less, however, you need to start asking a few questions, such as "What's the catch?" and "What *don't* I get?" The answers to these questions can help you decide whether you want to stay in the $500 bracket or move up a notch. Following are some of the typical drawbacks of going cheap:

- **Monitor not included:** Most PCs in the sub-$500 range don't include the monitor. Plan on spending at least $200 for a monitor.

- **Online service agreement required:** To offset the cost of the PC, many online service providers (such as Prodigy and CompuServe) agree to help dealers slash PC prices in exchange for the customer's commitment to pay for a two- or three-year subscription to the service (a $500 to $700 commitment).

- **Less-powerful processor:** Sub-$500 PCs typically use processors that are a generation behind the latest processors. Although sufficient for most word-processing tasks, these processors are not designed for the latest multimedia software and games.

- **Insufficient memory (RAM):** The 32 megabytes of RAM that come in most PCs in the sub-$500 range is the least amount of memory that a PC needs to even wake up in the morning. For most uses, a PC needs at least 64 megabytes of RAM to effectively run multiple programs and programs that rely heavily on graphics and animation.

- **Low-capacity hard drive:** The two- to four-gigabyte hard drive that most low-end PCs contain may seem large at first, but after you install a bunch of programs, cruise the Internet for a couple weeks, and start churning out documents, you quickly run out of storage space.

- **Second-rate video:** A good video-display card can perk up any PC by handling the job of generating images on the monitor. Manufacturers commonly cut costs by using an integrated (nonupgradeable) display card or by installing a cheap card that uses the PC's memory and processing power instead of its own, thus slowing down the PC.

- **Few expansion options:** Inexpensive PCs are typically disposable by design, offering virtually no way to add a new disk drive, modem, or additional memory or to upgrade obsolete components. If your computing needs grow (and they will), you have no way to improve the PC.

For low-cost desktop PCs, check out eMachines by visiting its Web site at www.e4me.com or by calling (877) 566-3463.

$500 to $1,000

The $500 to $1,000 price range is where things start to get interesting . . . and a little easier. A PC in this price bracket typically includes a monitor. The dealer may even throw in a low-end printer and a service agreement!

For less than a thousand bucks, however, don't count on getting a Pentium III processor, gobs of memory, an enormous hard drive, or a big-screen monitor. These machines are still basic PCs, but they pack enough punch for most users. Table 2-2 lists the typical components that you find in PCs in the sub-$1,000 price range.

Table 2-2: What You Can Get for Less Than $1,000

Component/Software	Specification/Offering
Processor MHz processor	Celeron, Cyrix, or AMD 300 to 400
Memory	32MB RAM
Hard drive	4GB
Modem or network card	56 Kbps modem (family PCs) or a network card (business PCs)
Removable storage drive	Floppy drive, 24 to 40X CD-ROM

(continued)

Table 2-2: What You Can Get for Less Than $1,000 (continued)

Component/Software	Specification/Offering
Monitor	SVGA 15-inch color
Input devices	Keyboard, mouse
Audio	Stereo sound card and speakers
Operating system	Windows 98
E-mail	Outlook
Web browser	Internet Explorer
Software	Home office or Works suite, anti-virus utility

The major problem with most of these sub-$1000 PCs is that they're likely to become obsolete in one to two years and can prove tough to upgrade, depending on where the manufacturer decides to cut corners. Dealers can also shave $400 to $500 off the list price by requiring you to subscribe to an online service for three years at a cost of more than $20 per month.

Before grabbing the first bargain that floats your way, read Chapters 3 and 4 to find out how to read between the lines and become a savvy shopper.

$1,000 to $2,000

As you cross the $1,000 threshold, you definitely leave Bargain Land behind. Most PCs in this price range are solid achievers with good track records and can grow (via upgrades) as your needs change.

Even at the low-end of this range ($1,200 to $1,300), you can get a PC with just about everything you need: a Pentium III processor, 64 megabytes of RAM, a 17-inch monitor and killer display card, a six-gigabyte hard drive, a speedy (24X or faster) CD-ROM drive, a stereo sound card and speakers, a 56 Kbps modem, and a nice collection of software to get you going.

PC package deals in this price range may not include some important accessories, such as a printer, a separate drive for backing up your files, a joystick, or a scanner (for copying photos and printed documents), but such a package is good to start with if you want a PC that's going to serve your needs two or three years down the road.

If you're looking for a bargain PC game machine, this price range is the one to consider. With a fast CD-ROM drive, a quality sound board, and a display card with four to eight megabytes of RAM (for storing the complex graphic instructions), a $1,000 to $2,000 PC can handle nearly any PC game currently on the market.

$2,000 to $3,000

For the price of a pretty good used car, you can purchase a top-of-the-line PC. At this price point, you're essentially cranking your PC up a notch from the $1,000 to $2,000 bracket. Every major PC component is better in this price range, as the following list describes:

■ You move up from a Pentium III 450 MHz processor to a 500 MHz or faster processor to boost performance.

■ You typically see double the memory — 128 megabytes of RAM instead of 64 megabytes. This additional memory gives your PC a real performance boost for running multiple programs, working with complex graphics, or playing games or video clips.

■ The monitor is typically larger (19 inches rather than 17 inches) or of a higher quality or both.

■ Instead of a PCI (Peripheral Connect Interconnect) display card, which is pretty fast, you get an AGP (Accelerated Graphics Port) display card, which is twice as fast. In addition, the standard four to eight megabytes of video RAM typically doubles to eight to 16 MB in such cards. These improvements help the display keep up with the rest of the PC.

■ Instead of a standard CD-ROM drive, PCs in this range may offer a combination DVD/CD-ROM drive. (A DVD disc can hold more than 17 times the amount of data as a CD, making them great for storing full-length movies, multimedia encyclopedias, and other media that otherwise require a stack of CDs to store.)

■ The sound system is better, typically featuring a 64-bit sound board and a speaker system with a subwoofer. With 64-bit sound, the PC starts inching into the range of true 3D audio to blast out those bone-shaking, movie-theater sound effects that make your PC games so enjoyable.

■ Instead of a standard 56 Kbps modem, the dealer typically upgrades the modem by adding fax and voice capabilities or by offering an ISDN, DSL, or cable modem. (ISDN, DSL, and cable modems, however, are not big pluses unless your phone or cable company offers these services in your area and you plan on paying a premium for higher Internet connection speeds.) You learn more about your modem options in chapters 4 and 7.

■ A color inkjet printer may come with the system, or if not, you can usually add one for less than $200 and still remain well within the $2,000 to $3,000 bracket.

In short, by shelling out an extra five hundred to a thousand bucks, you get a PC that's faster right now and lasts without an upgrade for at least three years.

In considering the type of modem that you want, ask your phone company and cable company about the Internet services they offer in your area and get a price quote. Don't buy a modem that you can't use.

More than $3,000

Any PC costing more than $3,000 is a powerhouse. Desktop PCs in this range typically offer a Pentium III 600 MHz processor or faster; 128 megabytes or more of RAM; a 19- or 21-inch monitor; an AGP display card with 16 to 32 megabytes of video RAM; a TV tuner card; a fast, 20+-gigabyte hard drive; a combination DVD/CD-ROM drive (and perhaps a CD-ROM drive that you can use to *write* data to CDs); a digital audio card with theater-quality speakers; and plenty of room to install additional components and drives later.

Notebook PCs in this price range are comparable to desktop PCs that fall in the $1,000 to $2,000 range, featuring a Pentium II or Celeron processor, a 14- or 15-inch AGP display, 64 to 96 megabytes of RAM, a six-gigabyte hard drive, a 24X CD-ROM drive, and a 56 Kbps modem.

If you just won the lottery, I recommend that you shop in this price bracket. Those of you who're far less fortunate should steer clear of this price range. You pay a premium for cutting-edge technology that's typically not worth the price. You can shave $500 off the asking price simply by choosing a slightly slower processor and a smaller hard drive, and you can't tell the difference.

CHAPTER 3
AVOIDING COMMON PITFALLS

IN THIS CHAPTER

- Passing up the first PC that you see
- Distinguishing between price and value
- Avoiding deals that seem too good to be true
- Questioning the advice of "knowledgeable" sales people
- Accounting for quality service and support

Buying a new PC is like purchasing a car from a Saturn dealer. With the current PC price wars, the markup on new PCs is only about five percent, fostering a no-haggle relationship between the PC dealer and you, the customer. In some ways, this no-haggle relationship is refreshing. You don't need to negotiate, and the salesperson can't jack up the price (at least not all that much).

Inspired by the stiff competition in the PC market, however, manufacturers and dealers manage to devise all sorts of creative ways to stick it to the customer. They may require you to sign up for a three-year subscription to an online service, entice you with an obsolete printer, or dangle a bunch of software in front of your nose to get you to buy an old model. Even more sinister, they may cut corners inside the PC by using low-quality components or by limiting your upgrade options.

The information in this chapter can help you avoid falling for these subtle scams and keep your focus on the best, most affordable PC for your needs.

Buying the First PC You See

After you finally decide to buy a PC, you may want to just drive over to the nearest computer or appliance store, walk through the aisles, and plop down a thousand bucks for what *looks* like a high-quality PC. After all, you play with the PC for five minutes, and it seems a *whole* lot better than your neighbor's computer.

Avoid the temptation and tuck that credit card right back into your wallet or purse. The PC that catches your eye may be the one for you, but until you examine the PC's specifications and do a little comparative analysis, as I explain in Chapter 4, you don't know what's inside that PC or how it stacks up to other PCs in its class. It may look fast and cool on the surface but be full of components that are rapidly flying down the high-tech highway to obsolescence.

Tip

Before you purchase from a retail store, always check current magazine ads and reviews to determine any recent advances in PC technology. And contact the manufacturer of the PC and ask whether the company has any newer models of the PC that you're considering purchasing. (Get the toll-free number from the salesperson or your handy-dandy magazine ad.)

Buying the Most Expensive PC

You don't need a backhoe to plant tomatoes. Nor do you need a PC with a Pentium III 600 MHz processor and an AGP display card to type letters and send e-mail. Don't let your hunger for power suck you into buying more PC than you need.

Stick to the hardware requirements that you calculated in Chapter 1 and focus on finding an affordable PC that can run the desired software efficiently. The money that you save comes in handy for purchasing additional software, installing a second phone line, obtaining office equipment and supplies, and doing something human, such as dining out at a four-star restaurant.

You probably have less to spend on a PC than you think. Factor in the cost of a desk or work center, a comfortable chair, a surge suppressor (for protecting your PC against lightning bolts), paper, printer cartridges, additional programs, and about $20 per month for an online or Internet service.

Buying the Cheapest PC

The $299 computer shown in Figure 3-1 looks like a good deal, and you may even love your bargain PC for the first few months you use it, but after the honeymoon is over, you start to notice some subtle problems: Programs may start to lock up because of insufficient memory. You may see a `Disk Full` error message whenever you try to install a program or save a document. Or if you attempt to update your software, you may find that its new hardware requirements are far beyond anything that your PC can handle.

No problem — you just upgrade your PC, right? Well, not exactly. Most manufacturers don't build cheap PCs with any foresight; they build them to sell. You open the case to plug in more memory, and you find that all the memory sockets are full. Or you decide to add a second hard drive, only to realize that you have no room to park it inside the case. Pretty soon, that sweet deal starts tasting pretty sour.

Figure 3-1: A bargain PC may end up costing you more in the long run.

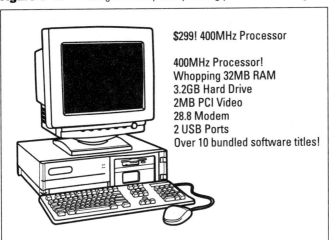

$299! 400MHz Processor

400MHz Processor!
Whopping 32MB RAM
3.2GB Hard Drive
2MB PCI Video
28.8 Modem
2 USB Ports
Over 10 bundled software titles!

To avoid this common pitfall, focus on value rather than price. Keep an eye on the PC requirements list that you compose in Chapter 1 and don't settle for anything less.

If a dealer advertises a PC as an "unbelievable deal," it probably is. A cheap PC can cost incredible amounts of money in the long run and cause you pangs of frustration for the entire time you own it.

Following a Salesperson's Advice

By following the instructions in this book, you have more knowledge about the PC market than do 90 percent of the salespeople you're likely to talk to. You also become aware of tradeoff issues and of the subtle ways that companies trim manufacturing costs — and, most important, you gain a thorough knowledge of how *you* plan to use the PC now and in the future.

In addition, salespeople have their own agenda. Their primary goal is to sell you a PC, *any* PC — not necessarily the PC that's right for you. Salespeople may be under pressure to push overstocked models that are fast becoming obsolete. Many retail stores cut deals with manufacturers to purchase PCs in high volume. If those PCs don't sell, they sit on the shelves or in a warehouse just waiting for some suckers to buy them.

To avoid falling prey to sales pitches, use the following strategies:

- Listen to the salespeople and take notes. Some of the information that they provide can prove very useful. For example, a salesperson may introduce you to a software program you hadn't considered or point out problems with some of the competitor's PCs.

- Check advertisements to see whether other dealers are offering the same (or a better) PC for less money.

- Call the PC manufacturer and ask whether the company has a later model on the market. (If you have access to the Internet, check out the manufacturer's Web site.) You learn more about researching your purchase in Chapter 5.

- Even if the PC that the salesperson recommends looks right for you, walk away and think about it, no matter how loud your kids scream, "Mommy and Daddy, buy this one!"

Limiting Your Future Upgrade Options

Can the PC you buy today handle your computing needs next year? How about the year after that? PC technology changes rapidly over time. Programs become bigger and more complex, games become more sophisticated, and multimedia files demand more power. To ensure that the PC you purchase can keep up with these changes, make sure that you can upgrade it by installing additional or improved components.

One of the subtlest ways that PC companies cut manufacturing costs is to trim the upgrade options, making it nearly impossible to improve the system later on. The following sections will help you spot and avoid these tricks.

Packed RAM slots

PC ads typically boast about the amount of RAM (memory) in a PC, but they fail to mention how the manufacturer installed the RAM. Most PCs contain four to six RAM sockets into which you plug memory cards, known as *SIMMs* (Single Inline Memory Modules). The PC ad may state that the PC has 64MB RAM, which is pretty good . . . assuming that the manufacturer installed the 64MB RAM as two 32MB modules. Such a configuration leaves two RAM sockets open for installing additional RAM later.

If the manufacturer installed the 64MB RAM as four 16MB SIMMs, the RAM occupies all the sockets, as shown in Figure 3-2. To install additional RAM, you must extract two 16MB modules to make room for higher-capacity modules. Though easy to do, you pay for 32MB of RAM you're not able to use. Always ask about the RAM's exact configuration and how much RAM you can add without removing existing modules.

Most current processors require a 64-bit path (a 64-lane highway) to the RAM. SIMMs are 32-bit, so you must install them in pairs to achieve the 64-bit requirement. DIMMs (Dual Inline Memory Modules), which are more expensive, are 64-bit, so you can upgrade RAM by installing a single DIMM. However, the PC must have DIMM RAM sockets.

Figure 3-2: If RAM modules currently occupy all the sockets, adding RAM later is more costly.

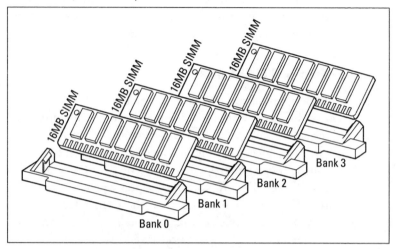

Few open expansion slots

Every PC component — the processor, RAM, disk drives, system clock, and so on — connects to a big circuit board known as the *motherboard*. On the motherboard you see long outlets, known as *expansion slots*, into which you can plug smaller circuit boards, known as *expansion boards* or *expansion cards*.

Make sure that the PC comes with several open (unoccupied) expansion slots. Table 3-1 lists and describes the various types of expansion slots. Most PCs come with both ISA and PCI slots; newer PCs include an additional expansion slot (the AGP slot) to support the latest display cards.

Table 3-1: **Open Expansion Slot Requirements**

Expansion Slot Type	Number Needed	Why I Need These
ISA	1-2	PCs use ISA (Industry Standard Architecture) slots for some slower expansion boards, including modems, network cards, and some sound boards.
PCI	3-4	PCs use PCI (Peripheral Connect Interconnect) slots for most expansion boards, including modems, most sound boards, and TV tuner cards.
AGP	1	PCs use AGP (Accelerated Graphics Port) for top-of-the-line display cards. If the PC comes with an AGP display card, you don't need a second AGP slot. If the PC has a PCI display card, make sure that it has an AGP expansion slot so that you can upgrade your display card later.

With the growing popularity of USB (Universal Serial Bus) ports, expansion slots may become less important. (*Ports* are outlets typically located on the back of the PC for plugging in a printer, monitor, keyboard, and so on.) You can plug up to 127 devices into a single USB port, including a keyboard, a joystick, a monitor, or a modem. Make sure that your PC comes with at least two USB ports.

Be careful when counting expansion slots. A common mistake is to count the metal plates that cover the expansion slot openings in the PC case. Some cases have more openings than the motherboard has expansion slots. Make sure that the ad or specification sheet specifies the number of open expansion slots.

Integrated components

In quality PCs, you plug the display card, modem, and sound card into expansion slots. If a better device becomes available, you can pop out the old device, plug in the new one, and you're ready to roll.

In cheaper PCs (with integrated components), the manufacturer solders some or all of these important devices to the motherboard as permanent fixtures and includes few expansion slots. If you need to upgrade a component, you must replace the entire motherboard. Watch out for PCs that feature integrated audio, video, or modem.

No open drive bays

Most PCs have four or more *drive bays* (parking spaces) that the manufacturer uses to mount the hard drive, floppy drive, CD-ROM drive, or other drives. If drives occupy all the bays, you're going to have a tough time adding a second hard drive later. Your only option becomes to attach an external drive via cable, and such a connection significantly reduces the speed at which data travels between the PC and disk drive.

Make sure that your PC has at least one open *full-height* drive bay — and preferably two. (A full-height drive bay can accommodate one full-height or two half-height drives.)

Drive bays may also be completely enclosed in the PC (internal) or hidden by a removable cover plate (external). You can install a hard drive in either bay type, but you must install an external drive, such as a floppy, backup, or CD-ROM drive in an external drive bay.

Low power supply

Inside every PC is a little box that supplies power to the processor, RAM, expansion slots, disk drives, and other components. This power supply typically delivers 150 to 300 watts.

PC manufacturers sometimes trim costs by using power supplies on the low end of this range. This practice doesn't cause any problems at first, but after you start adding RAM, a second hard drive, and a turbocharged display card, your PC's thirst for power may start exceeding the amount that the power supply can produce. A low power supply can eventually cause your PC to lock up unexpectedly and even damage sensitive components.

Use Table 3-2 to determine the power supply needs for typical desktop PCs.

Table 3-2:   Power Supply Recommendations

PC Type	Power Supply Rating
Standard desktop	150 to 200 watts
Minitower	200 to 250 watts
Full tower	250 to 300 watts

Power supply ratings are rarely advertised or even stuck to the outside of the PC (where they might do some good). Ask the dealer for a specifications sheet that includes the power supply rating.

Getting Hooked by the Software Bundle

Whenever a PC dealer offers you a huge bundle of free software with the purchase of a new PC, watch your wallet. The dealer is trying to do one of the following two things:

- Entice you to buy an obsolete PC by offering you a bunch of software

- Make the PC seem like more of a value compared to competitive PCs by offering old or unpopular programs that the dealer picked up for cheap

Although free software is nice, never purchase less PC than you need just to get some. Compare prices and systems carefully. If two dealers are offering the same PC for the same price but one is throwing in some extra software, picking the PC with the free software makes sense. Otherwise, go for the better PC with the more attractive price tag.

All PCs come with operating system software such as Windows 98 or Windows 2000. Most PCs also include a suite of applications, such as Microsoft Office or Microsoft Home Essentials.

Overlooking Service and Support

Contrary to what most computer professionals say, using a PC is not as easy as working a VCR (not that using a VCR's real easy either). I've been working with PCs for more than 10 years, and I still experience the occasional *Twilight Zone* tragedy. I recently installed a program, restarted my PC — and a completely blank screen greeted me. I resolved the problem, but it made me realize just how shocking such an incident could be to a first-time PC user.

When you're buying your first PC and just getting started in the world of personal computing, don't try to go it alone. Make sure that the dealer is going to stick with you during your first year. Any reputable dealer offers at least the following with any PC purchase:

- **One-year warranty:** The manufacturer should repair any faulty equipment for free for at least one year. Better PC manufacturers offer a three-year warranty. Find out if you must mail the PC back to the manufacturer for repairs or if you can take it into a local certified technician (which is much better).

- **Telephone and online support:** Does the manufacturer or dealer offer free phone support? For how long? Full 24-hour support, including weekends, is best — catastrophes rarely occur during convenient hours. If the dealer has a Web site with a technical support area, that's a real plus, too.

- **On-site service:** Although I'm not one to recommend service contracts, I do recommend that you pay a little extra for on-site service. Trust me — you don't want to pack up a desktop PC, ship it to the manufacturer, and then wait two weeks for the repairs.

Some manufacturers send you a loaner while repairing your equipment, but disconnecting, packing, and shipping devices back to a manufacturer — and then doing it all again after you receive your repaired equipment — is still a hassle.

CHAPTER 4

TRACKING DOWN THE BEST DEAL

Now that you know what you want and are a little more skeptical about what's available, you can start doing some serious shopping for PCs and narrow your choices.

In this chapter, you learn how to translate a typical PC advertisement into plain English, spot red flags, and identify the subtle differences between comparable PCs. You also learn about the three best places to shop for your PC.

Scanning Advertisements

Whenever you come across a PC advertisement that catches your eye, save it. Knowledge is power, and the more that you know about what's currently on the market and at what prices, the more savvy a PC shopper you become. The following sections tell you what to look for in the different types of ads.

Reading the sales inserts in your Sunday paper

If you're thinking about purchasing a PC, resisting the PC ads in the Sunday newspaper is almost impossible. These full-color ads hold out the promise of powerful, fully equipped PCs at a fraction of the cost you'd pay anywhere else . . . surely a computer shopper's paradise.

As I'm writing this chapter, I'm looking at an ad for a $449.99 PC (the price appears in really big type) that includes a 400 MHz Celeron processor, 64MB RAM, a 6GB hard drive, a 32X CD-ROM drive, a 56 Kbps modem, an AGP display card with 11MB video RAM, stereo speakers, a 15-inch monitor, *and* a color printer. Who wouldn't buy this system?!

Well, here's the fine print: The total price is actually $1,029.99, but you subtract $100 for the manufacturer rebate, $50 for the monitor rebate, $30 for the printer rebate, and $400 for the Prodigy "Instant Savings Plan," which is more like a "Save Now, Pay Later" plan. (You must agree to use the Prodigy service for 3 years at a cost of $19.95 per month for a total of $718.20.) Here's what that bargain PC *really* costs:

$1,029.99
-$100.00
-$50.00
-$30.00
-$400.00
+$718.20
$1,168.19

That's still not a bad deal (assuming that the PC has the required upgrade options, which you can't tell from the ad), but it's a far cry from the advertised price of $449.99.

Flipping through computer magazines

Computer magazines, such as *PC Computing* or *FamilyPC*, contain numerous ads from mail-order companies and can prove useful for two reasons: They provide important information about current PC technology, and they give you a pretty good idea of what's a fair price.

Go to the library and flip through three consecutive issues of the same computer magazine. You notice that, with each passing month, you can get a better PC for less money.

Obtaining catalogues

Catalogues provide a bit more information than you get in an advertisement. A catalogue typically displays a clear picture of the PC and a detailed description, lists upgrade options, describes the major components, and explains your finance options.

If you come across an ad in a computer magazine and want more information, call the toll-free number that the ad provides and ask for a catalogue. Most mail-order companies are more than happy to add you to their mailing lists.

What's Inside Is What Counts: Deciphering PC Ads

Don't be surprised if your eye's glaze over as you start reading PC ads. They're packed with cryptic terms and abbreviations that make figuring out what you're getting or comparing one PC to another nearly impossible. Take a look at Figure 4-1 to see what I mean.

Figure 4-1: A typical PC ad.

Screamer 550 MHz PC!
Intel Pentium III, 550 MHz
128 MB SDRAM
11.0GB Ultra ATA Hard Drive
6X DVD-ROM Drive
8MB AGP Graphics
SoundBlaster AudioPCI 64D
GCS-200 Speakers
56K Internet/Fax Modem
17" monitor (15.9" Viewable)

If the ad looks like Egyptian hieroglyphics, don't worry. After you read the following sections, you can translate this ad as easily as King Tut.

Processors — what's the difference?

In the past, your processor choices were limited. You could buy a PC with an Intel 486 or an Intel Pentium (586). Now, the choices aren't so clear: Intel Pentium III, Xeon, Athlon, Celeron, AMD-K6-3, AMD-K6-2, Cyrix M II. The situation's confusing, and it's sure to get even more confusing as the battle of the processors heats up.

Check out Table 4-1 to help clear your head and make a wise decision, but keep in mind that processors are constantly in development and the information may be out of date by the time you read this book. Always check ads and reviews to obtain current information.

Table 4-1: Processor Comparisons

Processor	Description
Intel Pentium Xeon	A turbocharged Pentium II or III designed for workstations and network servers. This powerful processor is seldom used in desktop PCs.
AMD Athlon	AMD's latest processor holds a slight edge over Intel's Pentium III in speed tests and is comparable in price.
Intel Pentium III	Intel's PC powerhouse drives a good section of the desktop PC market. With the introduction of the Athlon, Pentium III prices should fall, making them a good buy.
AMD K6-3	AMD's answer to the Pentium III, this processor provides the power that most users need at a slightly lower price.
Intel Pentium II	A big step down in performance from the Pentium III, the Pentium II is still used in notebook PCs and low-end desktop PCs.
Intel Celeron	Intel designed its "bargain" processor to make its product competitive with lower-priced processors. Although Celeron systems are commonly advertised alongside Pentium III systems, the Celeron processor is more comparable to a Pentium II.
AMD K6-2	In the same family as the Pentium II and Celeron processors, the AMD K6-2 incorporates a more economical design to rival the Pentium II and Celeron in performance and beat it in price.
Cyrix M II	This one is the processor of choice for "free" and virtually free PCs. Although the Cyrix M II offers performance comparable to that of the Celeron and AMD K6-2, it is frequently used in bargain systems in which all components are a notch lower. Otherwise, it's a good value.

Processor speeds, such as 450 MHz and 600 MHz, are deceiving because they represent only the speed at which the processor is running, not its total production. For example, say you have two trucks: the first truck can carry 100 TVs at 50 miles an hour, and the other can carry 1000 TVs at 30 miles an hour. It's obvious that the bigger truck can move more TVs. Processor speeds mean little unless you consider other factors, such as how much data the processor can handle with each tick of the clock and the speed at which the processor communicates with the rest of the system.

In choosing a system, pick the processor type first and then consider speed. Decide whether you want a Pentium III or Athlon system, for example, and then decide whether you want the 450 MHz or the 600 MHz system.

RAM: Amount and speed

The more RAM (memory) a PC has, the more data that it can hold in its "brain" and the less often it must read stuff from the slower disk drive. For basic word processing and e-mail, 32MB RAM is sufficient. If you plan on using your PC for games or graphics or plan on keeping multiple programs running, don't settle for less than 64MB. And make sure that the RAM comes in the form of *SDRAM*, or *Sync-DRAM* (Synchronous Dynamic RAM), which is much faster than the old DRAM (*Dynamic* RAM).

Make sure that you can add RAM later without removing existing RAM modules. See Chapter 3 for more information.

Hard drive type, size, and speed

Although the storage capacity of the drive is of utmost importance, you want to shop for speed as well. A slow hard drive can drag down the overall performance of your PC. In comparing hard drives, use Table 4-2 as your guide.

Table 4-2: Hard Drive Specs

If Considering . . .	You Want to Get . . .
Size	5GB (gigabyte) or larger. If you're a gamer or a graphic artist, bump up the storage to 8-10GB. If you plan on doing a little video editing or digital photography, shop in the 20GB+ range.
Average seek time	Eight to 12 ms (milliseconds). This value represents the time the drive takes to move the read/write mechanism to a specific point on the disk. The smaller the number, the faster the drive. Although a couple of milliseconds doesn't seem like much, if the disk drive lags behind, the processor has to wait, and overall system performance suffers.
Spindle speed	Measured in RPMs (revolutions per minute), the speed at which the disk spins inside the drive. 5400 is standard; 7200 is common in high-end systems.
Transfer rate	33 Mbps (megabytes per second). This rate represents the amount of data that the drive can send to the PC per second. The higher the number, the faster is the drive. This is the most important rating for a hard drive.
Disk cache	512KB is standard; more is better. The *disk cache* is a temporary storage area on the drive that quickly supplies data to the PC without needing to access the disk itself. Make sure the drive has its own cache instead of using a portion of the PC's RAM.
Drive type	Ultra ATA (*AT Attachment*), a step up from EIDE (*Enhanced Intelligent Drive Electronics*) drives, features a 33 Mbps transfer rate. Ultra ATA drives are very practical and affordable. For better performance, look for an ATA/66 or DMA/66 drive. (DMA is short for Direct Memory Access, a specification supported in ATA/66 drives. See Chapter 8 for more information.)

PCI or AGP graphics?

A PC's monitor plugs into a display adapter that generates images on the screen. Most new PCs use either a PCI (Peripheral Connect Interconnect) or an AGP (Accelerated Graphics Port) display adapter.

Which is better? AGP wins, hands down. It can send data to the monitor twice as fast as the older PCI adapters can. Make sure that the card comes with at least 4MB of VRAM (video RAM). VRAM enables the adapter to store more instructions, freeing your primary RAM for other tasks and enabling instructions to pass more quickly from the adapter to the monitor.

Monitors: Size and clarity

You don't want to shell out extra money for a first-rate display adapter, only to plug in a second-rate monitor. Make sure that the monitor matches the following profile:

■ **Size:** The 15-inch monitor is on its way out, and 17 inches is now the standard; 19 inches is great if you can afford it. (Compare the "viewable area," not just the tube size, as shown in Figure 4-2.) LCD (flat-screen) monitors cost more, but they provide a larger viewable area; a 15-inch LCD, for example, is nearly equivalent to a standard 17-inch monitor.

■ **Resolution:** You want 1024-by-768 dpi (dots per inch) or higher. Higher resolutions enable the monitor to display objects smaller and fit more information on-screen.

■ **Dot pitch:** You need .28 for a 15-inch monitor, .26 for a 17-inch monitor, and .25 for a 19-inch monitor. *Dot pitch* represents the space between the dots that make up the display. In general, the smaller the dot pitch, the sharper the image. (Dot pitch is frequently displayed in ads, but you may need to ask the dealer.)

■ **Refresh rate:** Look for 75 Hz for 15- or 17-inch monitors and 85 Hz for larger monitors. If the refresh rate is lower than 75 Hz, the monitor may have an imperceptible flicker that can harm your vision and give you headaches (or a perceptible flicker that can drive you crazy).

Figure 4-2: Compare the viewable area, not the tube size.

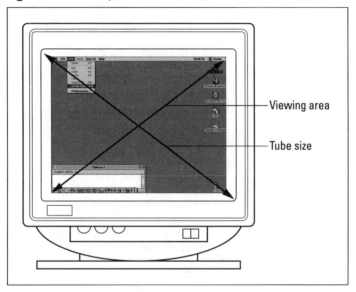

Viewing area

Tube size

Some monitors come with built-in speakers and a microphone, which look pretty cool and save you some space. The sound quality is usually substandard, however, upgrades are difficult, and if the speaker blows, you have to take your monitor in for repairs.

Sound boards and other audio specs

Your new PC can double as a boom box, but how well it blasts out audio clips depends on the sound card and speakers. Table 4-3 shows you what to look for in a quality PC stereo system.

Table 4-3:   What to Look for in PC Audio

In Looking at . . .	Settle for No Less than . . .
Fidelity	16-bit 44.1 kHz (kilohertz). This setup matches the standards for audio CDs.
Output	Wavetable audio. Wavetable technology enables developers to digitize real-world sounds so that a PC can play them.
Speakers	10 watts or higher. Sound from the best sound card on the market sounds lousy if you play it through low-quality speakers.
Games and DVD	Subwoofer. The subwoofer ensures high-quality, bone-shaking bass output that makes DVD movies and some PC games more enjoyable (or so they say).
Games	Game port. Most sound cards include a game port into which you can plug a joystick. If your PC has a separate game port, you don't need an extra one on the sound card.
Music composition	MIDI (Musical Instrument Digital Interface) port. This interface enables you to connect a musical instrument, such as a digital piano keyboard, to the sound card so that you can play and record compositions.

Many ads list a set of stereo speakers with a subwoofer as a 2.1 audio system (one speaker on each side of you and a sub-woofer on the floor in front of you). They describe surround sound as a 5.1 system (four speakers around you, one in front, and a subwoofer on the floor).

Modem madness (and confusion)

To make the modem choice very simple, take this advice: Get a PC with an internal 56 Kbps V.90 modem — and don't worry what V.90 stands for. This standard modem supports a relatively fast and affordable connection to most online and Internet services. If you want more out of your 56 Kbps modem, look for the following features:

■ **Fax support:** Fax support enables you to send and receive faxes by using your PC.

■ **Voice support:** With voice support, you can use your computer as an answering machine — people can leave voice messages while you're away from your computer. You can also use your modem as a speakerphone.

You may also consider the following alternatives to the standard 56 Kbps modem (but before you do, call your phone and cable-TV companies to determine which services are available in your area and ask the folks at your online or Internet service whether the service supports these high-speed connections):

■ **ISDN:** Short for *I*ntegrated *S*ervices *D*igital *N*etwork, ISDN transfers data digitally across special phone lines at up to 128 Kbps.

■ **DSL:** Short for *D*igital *S*ubscriber *L*ine, DSL transfers data digitally across standard phone lines at up to 8 Mbps (megabits per second), or approximately 35 times faster than a standard 56 Kbps modem. This option is an expensive one that's not widely available, but PC dealers are always happy to sell you a DSL modem.

■ **Cable:** Assuming that your cable company offers cable Internet service, you can use a cable modem to access this service for a very fast Internet connection (at 3 to 4 Mbps). Setup fees and monthly service, however, can prove very expensive.

■ **Satellite:** For a couple hundred bucks up front and about a buck for every hour you're online, you can stick a satellite dish on your roof and get a pretty fast Internet connection (400 Kbps).

A *WinModem*, or Windows Modem, relies on the system's processor to process data rather than using its own processor. This setup slightly reduces the price, but it also reduces the overall performance of the modem and the PC itself.

Reading Between the Lines

What an ad doesn't tell you is often more important than what it does tell you. The ad shown in Figure 4-1, for example, has no information about the number of open expansion slots or unoccupied drive bays, the monitor's dot pitch, or how many RAM sockets are open.

If you become seriously interested in a particular PC, read the ad with this chapter open and compose a list of questions for the dealer. Then call the dealer and fill in the missing information. Ask the dealer whether specifications sheets (spec sheets) are available. Most manufacturers print up spec sheets that provide detailed information about the installed components, including the power supply rating, hard drive type, and the number and type of RAM sockets.

Examining the Fine Print

Every PC ad overflows with footnote asterisks, crosses, and numbers that point to a fine-print section. Get your magnifying glass and read the fine print. Here's where you learn what the sticker price *doesn't* include, what the warranty excludes, and whether you must sign up for a three-year subscription to an online service.

CHAPTER 5
DOING YOUR HOMEWORK

IN THIS CHAPTER

- Finding the best place to buy a PC
- Reading current reviews in computer magazines
- Checking a dealer's background
- Getting advice from other computer buyers
- Keeping abreast of manufacturing defects and product alerts

In the "buyer-beware" PC market, the customer is responsible for locating a reliable dealer and a quality product. If you purchase a lemon from a shady Internet dealer, you're considered the sucker.

You can find plenty of places to purchase your new PC and a healthy supply of resources for evaluating products and merchants, but you must be willing to sniff around. You need to scan magazine articles, check the phone book, and wander the Web to find the best place to shop — and then do a thorough background check to make sure that you're buying a quality product from a reliable dealer.

This chapter acts as your PC buyer's research guide, pointing the way to the resources you need to become a savvy PC shopper.

Shopping Retail

Shopping for a PC at Best Buy, Circuit City, Office Depot, Sears, or Radio Shack, has its advantages. You get to roll the mouse around, peck at the keyboard, and watch images pop up on the monitor. And because these stores deal in high volume, they typically offer PCs at a reasonable price. However, you should take the following steps to ensure that you're getting the right PC for you at the right price:

1. Examine the PC's specifications, just as you would do if you were ordering through a mail-order company.

2. Ask about the store's return policy. If they won't let you return the PC, they probably won't help you when something goes wrong.

3. Ask about service and support. Does the store have an on-site service center? What's the average time it takes for repairs? Is there a minimum fee for repairs? Is there someone you can call if you run into problems?

Going Mail-Order

Mail-order companies, such as Compaq, Gateway, Dell, and Micron, sell more computers than all the retail stores combined. To stay competitive, they offer the latest technology at reasonable prices and typically back up their products with quality warranties, service, and support.

Many people hesitate to purchase from a mail-order company, thinking that all such companies are fly-by-night operations. This simply is not true. As long as you stick with a big-name company that has been in the business for three years or more, you have little to worry about.

Finding mail-order companies is not difficult. Just grab any PC magazine and start flipping through the pages. Once you have a general idea of what you want, call the toll-free number in the ad and talk to a salesperson.

When purchasing from a mail-order company, ask about shipping costs. Many companies that offer the lowest prices jack up the shipping costs.

Shopping Online

One of the best places to shop for a PC is on the Web. Visit a friend or relative who has a PC and an Internet connection and spend a couple hours meandering through PC dealer Web sites. (Your friend or relative can help you move around on the Web.) On these sites, you'll find the most up-to-date offerings, check out available options, and see immediately the total cost of the PC you want. See Figure 5-1.

Be as careful shopping online as you are when shopping from a mail-order company. Deal only with established merchants who have a good reputation and watch out for incredibly good deals. It's incredibly easy to put up a storefront on the Web and display some fancy order forms and pictures of Visa cards to look like a legitimate company.

Here's a list of the four most popular mail-order companies on the Web and the addresses you need to connect:

- **Gateway:** www.gw2k.com
- **Dell:** www.dell.com
- **Compaq:** www.compaq.com
- **Micron:** www.micronpc.com

Figure 5-1: You can "build" the PC you want and determine its total cost on the manufacturer's Web site.

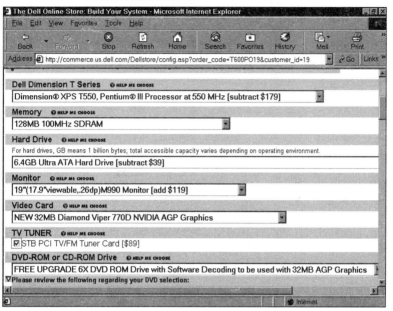

What About Used and Reconditioned PCs?

For your first PC, steer clear of used or reconditioned PCs, no matter how inexpensive they appear. I gave my dad a hand-me-down PC, and it nearly put an end to his computing career. He was constantly running out of disk space, receiving "Insufficient memory" messages, and learning that every program he wanted to use was incapable of running on the system.

Even reconditioned PCs that come with good warranties are rarely a bargain. The dealer might slap a powerful processor and a bigger hard drive in the PC, but the other components create insurmountable bottlenecks that prevent the new components from achieving top speed.

Start with a clean slate. Buy new.

Finding and Reading Reviews

Don't trust a dealer's ad to tell you how well a PC performs. A fast processor yoked to a slow hard drive and a scarcity of memory can be slower than a well-designed system built around a slower processor. You have only the following two ways of determining how well the PC performs as a unit

■ *Run benchmark tests on the PC.* Benchmark programs test the speed of each major component and the overall system performance.

■ *Read a review of the system.* Find one written by an impartial judge with access to benchmark programs.

The first option isn't very practical. If you're buying from a mail-order company, you have no way to run a series of benchmarks on the PC, even if you know how to do it. If you're shopping at retail stores, no salesperson is going to permit you to pop in a floppy disk and run a program that could potentially infect the machine with a virus.

Fortunately, PC magazines are full of PC reviews and awards for those systems that perform best. Pick up a copy of *PC Magazine*, *Computer Shopper*, or *Family PC* and read the PC and hardware reviews from cover to cover. Although reviews may spread the technical jargon a little thick, they typically provide a general thumbs up or thumbs down at the end that can help guide your decision. Reviews in magazines that cater to the novice, such as Family PC, are a little more down-to-earth.

Magazines also contain reviews for specific components, such as processors, sound boards, modems, display cards, and software. Don't skip these reviews. They may contain important information or warnings about a particular component of the PC.

Researching Manufacturers and Dealers

How can you tell whether a dealer stands behind its products and offers quality service after the sale? If the dealer offers a 30-day, money-back guarantee, does the dealer honor that guarantee? How available and competent is the dealer's technical support staff? Does the manufacturer have a reputation for producing high-quality products? Will the manufacturer back up the product with competent technical support and service?

Seeing the number of PC dealers that hawk their wares on the Internet, in newspapers and magazines, and on TV, you may begin to wonder which dealers are just trying to make a quick buck and which ones are reliable, customer-oriented companies trying to stay in business.

To distinguish the fly-by-nighters from legitimate businesses, you need to conduct a little research. The following sections tell you how to start.

Examine all return policies and warranties thoroughly *before* you buy.

Checking out the competition

Other than in reviews, you don't find many side-by-side comparisons of comparable PCs. Too many different brand-name PCs are on the market. If two or more dealers are offering comparable PCs at nearly the same price, however, calling each dealer and asking why you should buy that dealer's PC rather than the competitor's isn't a bad idea. You need to be skeptical of the advice, but dealers often do have access to valuable market news, such as whether the competitor is about to go belly up (making its three-year unlimited warranty a little less valuable).

Even more important in considering the competition is to look at the differences between installed devices. Is the Voodoo 3 video card better than the Matrox G400 or the RIVA TNT2? Is the Trinitron monitor worth an extra $100? In this area, you commonly find side-by-side comparisons in reviews and on the manufacturer's Web sites, as shown in Figure 5-2.

Figure 5-2:   Manufacturers commonly compare their products to the competition.

AMD - AMD Athlon(TM) Competitive Comparison - Microsoft Internet Explorer

File   Edit   View   Favorites   Tools   Help

Back   Forward   Stop   Refresh   Home   Search   Favorites   History   Mail   Print

Address http://www.amd.com/products/cpg/athlon/comparison.html

Home | Search | Contact Us

AMD   About AMD | Products | Support

Processor Architecture/Technology--Competitive Comparison

Feature	AMD Seventh Generation AMD Athlon™ (Slot A)	Intel Previous Generation Pentium® III (Slot 1)	AMD Previous Generation AMD-K6®-III (Super7™)
Operations per clock cycle	9	5	6
Integer pipelines	3	2	2
Floating point pipelines	3	1	1
Full x86 decoders	3	1	1
L1 cache size	128KB	32KB	64KB

Internet

Software packages, especially games, recommend a particular make and model of display card or sound board. Remember to check your hardware requirements list as you're looking at components.

PC manufacturers may use off-brand components (such as sound boards, modems, and monitors) to hold down the cost. Make sure the component manufacturers, as well as the PC manufacturer, are reliable. You may have trouble getting technical support for a sound board if the sound board manufacturer goes out of business.

Checking with the Better Business Bureau

You're tired of corporate America, and your rebellious nature draws you to the mom and pop computer store down the street or the no-name Internet dealer. Besides, that mom and pop store is offering an incredible deal on a killer PC. Should you throw some business its way?

Not before checking it out. Grab your handy-dandy telephone book and find the number of your local Better Business Bureau. Give it a call and ask whether any complaints have been filed against the dealer.

If you have an Internet connection, you can find a list of local branches of the Better Business Bureau at www.bbb.org/bureaus/index.html.

Identifying common warning signs

Most legitimate manufacturers and dealers aren't going to scam you. They know that your PC is going to be obsolete in three years, even if they sell you a top-of-the-line system, and they want your return business. So if you stick with big-name companies, such as Compaq, Hewlett Packard, IBM, Dell, and various others, you're fairly safe.

If you're purchasing an off-brand computer from a mail-order company or a custom PC from some small sweatshop down the street, however, look for the following warning signs:

■ **Unbelievable deals:** During the writing of this book, a mail-order company was offering $299 PCs, which it never shipped. The company failed to anticipate the number of orders it would receive, and it couldn't fill those orders. (I found this story on the Better Business Bureau's Web site.)

■ **Down payment required:** In another shady deal, an Internet dealer was offering cheap PCs to any sucker who'd send a down payment of $20.

■ **Credit cards not accepted:** As you learn in Chapter 9, a credit card is your best defense if you encounter problems with your PC. A good credit card company can provide the leverage you need when a dealer fails to deliver or delivers an unsatisfactory product. Never pay by cash or check.

■ **No address:** If the company doesn't provide its address, it's probably hiding from something.

■ **Billing at time of order:** Most legitimate dealers bill your credit card at the time it ships the PC. Always purchase from a dealer who bills you at the time it ships your order.

■ **Off-brand components:** Though an off-brand component may offer high-quality at a low price, the manufacturer of that component may not stay in business as long as an established, brand-name manufacturer.

■ **Requiring credit card information up front:** If you're ordering on the Internet, order only from those companies that provide a detailed invoice before asking you to enter your credit card number or shipping address.

■ **No technical support, warranty, or on-site service:** Such companies aren't about to back up their products.

Printed and online magazines try to prevent listing ads for illegitimate businesses. Before ordering from a company, see whether it has an ad in a magazine.

Seeking Recommendations

With so many people buying new PCs, you must know *someone* who's purchased a PC recently. Grill the person. Does the person like using the PC? If the person ordered it from a mail-order company, did the company ship the PC quickly and did it arrive in good condition? Did the person run into any problems? Did the dealer resolve the problems satisfactorily?

Nothing is better than a personal recommendation from a close friend or associate, especially one who's rarely satisfied with anything.

If none of your friends or associates use a PC, contact a local PC users group for recommendations. Techie types like to talk about their fabulous PCs, and if a shady company or a bad product burns them, they're even more willing to talk.

Checking Customer Satisfaction Ratings

You can't trust what a company says about how satisfied its customers are, nor can you solicit feedback with your own surveys. So how can you get honest testimonies from customers? The only way is to cruise the Web.

Several companies have sites set up where customers can post messages about their experiences with a particular product or merchant. You can pull up a list of those messages and read what people are saying. Assuming that you have an Internet connection or can use a friend's, check out the following sites:

■ *CNET Shopper*, at `www.shopper.com/rate/`, displays ratings for companies that advertise on CNET. Most of these companies are computer warehouses from which you can purchase complete systems, upgrade components, and software. (Keep in mind that the ratings may be a bit skewed by the fact that these companies advertise with CNET.)

■ *ConsumerReviews*, at `www.crev.com`, features reviews written by real-life customers for all sorts of merchandise, including PCs and computer games. This site is a great place for uncensored, heartfelt criticism.

■ *PC Magazine's Customer Ratings*, at `www.zdnet.com/pcmag/special/reliability98/index.html`, provide ratings for both merchants and products.

■ *BizRate.com*, at `www.bizrate.com`, is an independent company that uses customer feedback to rate various businesses that choose to list with BizRate (see Figure 5-3). (Makes you wonder whether you can trust the reviews.)

Figure 5-3: BizRate.com rates merchants.

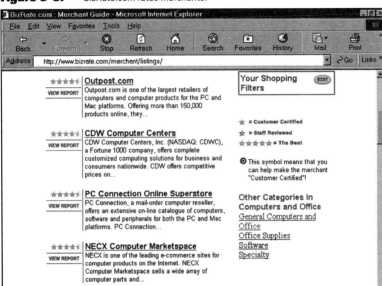

Tracking Down Product Alerts

About two years ago, I purchased a special disk drive for backing up files. Eleven months later, the drive sounded like a coffee grinder, and I couldn't recover my backup files. After checking out the manufacturer's Web site and some Internet newsgroups (message boards), I learned that just about everyone who purchased one of these overpriced lemons experienced the same problem. To avoid making a similar mistake, always do the following research before you buy:

■ Call the manufacturer or check its Web site to determine whether it's had any product recalls lately.

■ Check the technical-support area on the Web site to see whether it has an inordinate amount of information about the product. This could indicate that the company offers great technical support, or that a large number of users encounter problems with the product. Read the technical support questions and answers to judge for yourself.

■ Check out Internet newsgroups (or have a knowledge-able friend do it for you) to look for any posted messages about a particular merchant, manufacturer, or product.

Don't believe all the unfiltered customer comments that you read. Some users blame the PC for problems that programs cause or overreact if a company doesn't live up to unreasonable expectations.

CHAPTER 6

TEST-DRIVING PCS

IN THIS CHAPTER

- Getting some hands-on experience
- Key questions to ask a salesperson
- Finding a comfortable keyboard and mouse
- Evaluating audio and video quality
- Comparing PC speeds in the real world

Two years ago, I decided that I needed a notebook PC. I did all the required research; I read magazine reviews, checked out product comparisons on the Internet, did background checks on mail-order companies, and read the fine print. I found the perfect notebook PC for my needs and budget, so I ordered it. After it arrived, I was as happy as a new daddy.

Then my brother-in-law stopped by with his new notebook PC. I just had to check it out. The keys felt better. The display had virtually no glare. The mouse pointer glided smoothly across the screen, and programs leaped into action. It even looked cooler than mine. Thinking that he must have paid a thousand bucks more than I did (and secretly seeking solace), I asked him what he paid for his notebook. It cost $100 LESS! Arghhhh!

The point of this story is that you should always get your hands on a few PCs to make some real-life comparisons before you buy one, even if you ultimately decide to purchase your PC from a mail-order company.

Finding a Place to Try Before You Buy

Retail stores love to put their PCs on display. They add a third dimension to the PC shopping experience. Shoppers can roll the mouse around, peck away at the keyboard, and get dazzled by the video show. Retailers hope that, after the prospective buyer touches the right PC, that person establishes an inseparable bond with it.

Although you want to avoid bonding with the retailer's PCs, checking them out never hurts. Go to Sears, Best Buy, Circuit City, OfficeMax, Gateway, or whatever local PC dealers are in your area and play around with their PCs. The following sections tell you what to look for as you test-drive PCs.

Many retail stores have lousy display areas. Keyboards and mice may be in disrepair, monitors may need adjustment, and the PCs may not even be plugged in. Before you visit a store, call ahead and ask how many PC systems are on display and functional. Although this won't tell you if the equipment is in good repair, it does provide some indication of whether taking a trip to the store is worth your time.

Playing with the Mouse and Keyboard

The mouse and keyboard are the two primary tools that you use to talk to your PC. If you don't like the way they feel, you're not going to like using your PC.

You want a mouse to fit comfortably in your hand and respond well to your movements. Try a couple clicks and double-clicks (that is, clicking twice real fast). Are the buttons tough to press? Do they feel too loosey-goosey? Some mice have a wheel between the two buttons that you can roll to scroll and perform some other fancy tricks. You usually find that the wheel is pretty cool, even if it seems to get in your way at first.

Tip

If the mouse pointer "sticks" on-screen, instead of gliding, the mouse may just need cleaning. Don't assume that the mouse is defective. If you like everything else about the mouse, ask the salesperson to try a new mouse.

In the past, keyboards offered few options. You could get a keyboard with keys that clicked (which I prefer) or one with a more "squishy" feel to it (with "silent" keys). Modern keyboards offer many more options that you need to consider, as the following list describes:

- **Comfort:** The most important consideration is still the feel of the keyboard. Are the spaces between the keys far enough apart? Is it easy to type on?

- **Ergonomic designs:** Ergonomic keyboards are curved to help you keep your wrists in a more natural position as you type. You don't have to rotate your wrists inward as far to make your fingers parallel to the keys. I never did like standard ergonomic keyboards, but I have a keyboard that I can split in half and adjust each half to a 45-degree angle with my desk, which I love.

- **Internet keyboards:** For quick Internet navigation, Internet keyboards feature hot buttons that you can press to access your favorite Web pages and enter common Web browser commands, such as Back and Forward (see Figure 6-1).

- **Wireless keyboards:** Typically using radio-frequency waves, these keyboards enable you to sit back and type without stretching a cord. Some of these wireless keyboards work better than others. Try before you buy.

- **USB keyboards:** If you purchase a PC with a USB port or two, you have the option of using a keyboard that connects to the USB port rather than to a standard PS/2 keyboard port. Though USB keyboards are slightly more expensive, some USB keyboards have additional USB ports, making the keyboard act as a USB *hub* into which you can plug additional USB devices.

■ **Keyboard/mouse combinations:** Some keyboards may include a touchpad or integrated mouse. If the keyboard includes a touchpad, make sure that it's positioned off to the side and not right under your thumbs.

Avoid keyboards that have mice connected to them. You usually need to replace your mouse long before you replace the keyboard.

Figure 6-1:   An Internet keyboard features buttons to enhance Web navigation.

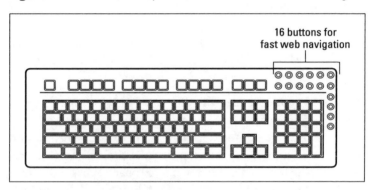

Checking the Video Display

You don't buy a TV set without glancing at a few picture tubes (a.k.a. *Cathode Ray Tubes* or CRTs), nor should you ever purchase a monitor before carefully examining the crispness of the image it displays. After all, you're going to stare at this thing the entire time that you're using your PC.

What should you look for? Image quality is the main consideration. The entire viewing area should display a consistently clear image. Examine the edges of the viewing area for fuzziness. On curved screens, check for any bowed lines or distortion. Curved screens are also more prone to causing glare.

Be kind to your eyes and check for glare and flicker. If the screen seems to flicker even slightly, move on to the next monitor. To check for glare, take along a pocket flashlight and perform the following steps:

1. Turn off the monitor to get a black screen.

2. Shine your flashlight at the screen from different angles while looking directly at the screen (as if you were using it).

3. Repeat the preceding steps on several different monitors.

Quality antiglare monitors absorb the light, reflecting back only a dim, fuzzy ball. Monitors with a glare problem look as though someone's inside the monitor pointing a flashlight at you. Glare can be a serious problem, especially if you plan on housing your PC in a room with a view.

You also want to consider the controls on the monitor. Are they easily accessible? You shouldn't need a screwdriver to adjust the brightness, contrast, and other display qualities. A monitor that connects to a USB port is also a plus, assuming that you purchase a PC with USB ports.

Flat-screen (LCD) displays provide superior image quality with less glare and flicker but carry a heftier price tag, often as much as $700 extra.

Checking the Audio Output

If you're a serious gamer or plan on watching action flicks on your PC, you should check out the audio system by cranking up the volume a bit. This provides you with important information, such as whether the speakers are powerful enough to withstand the sound board's output. To test the audio system, take the following steps:

1. Bring along your own audio CD or DVD (Digital Video Disc) movie or ask the salesperson for a loaner.

2. Pop the disc in the drive. If it doesn't start playing, ask the salesperson for help.

3. If the speakers have volume controls, crank them up slightly beyond the comfort level.

4. If the sound board has a volume control, crank that up a little, too. (You may need to reach around the back of the PC.)

5. If you still don't get the desired volume, double-click the little speaker icon in the lower right corner of the screen and then drag all the volume controls to the top (see Figure 6-2).

After you turn up the volume, listen for the following signs of a poor audio system: cracking sounds, muffled treble, no bass, and static. Make sure that the speakers produce stereo output.

Remember

If you're shopping for a PC with a DVD player, make sure that you get a good sound system to accompany it. Otherwise, you can't experience the full effects of DVD movies.

Figure 6-2: You can control the volume from Windows.

┌ Drag the volume control to the top

Volume Control						_ □ ×
Options Help						
Volume Control	Wave	MIDI	CD Audio	Line-In	Microphone	
Balance:	Balance:	Balance:	Balance:	Balance:	Balance:	
Volume:	Volume:	Volume:	Volume:	Volume:	Volume:	
☐ Mute all	☐ Mute	☐ Mute	☐ Mute	☐ Mute	☐ Mute	

SB16 Mixer [220]

Avoid battery-powered speaker systems. Look for AC-powered speakers (speakers that you can plug into an outlet).

Speed Can Be Deceiving

Although retail stores are the best place to compare mice, keyboards, monitors, and audio systems, they're the worst place to compare system speeds. Just too many variables affect a PC's speed: the types and number of programs it's running, how long the PC's been on, goofy stuff other shoppers do to the PC, and so on. To perform a valid comparison, take the following steps on any two PCs that you want to compare:

1. Ask the salesperson to shut down and restart both PCs. Doing so closes all programs and gives each PC a fresh start.

2. Ask the salesperson to shut down any screen savers or other programs that may be running in the background.

3. Run the same program on each PC. For example, click the Start button (lower left corner of the screen), point to Programs, Accessories, and Games, and then click Solitaire.

Talking to a Salesperson

The quality of the salespeople you meet varies. I've visited PC and electronic stores knowing full well what I wanted and absolutely sure that the store carried what I wanted only to be told by some ignorant, bull-headed salesperson that the store didn't carry the product. I've also talked with salespeople who taught me a lesson or two about PCs.

In talking to a salesperson, you need to establish two things: First, does the person know anything? Second, can the person convey the differences between PCs in the store's product line? To get the help that you need (or to determine that this person can't help you), start with general questions and then get down to the details, as the following list demonstrates:

■ If you were buying a PC, which one would you buy? Why?

■ What kind of PC do you own?

■ What's the difference between a Pentium III processor and an Athlon? Which is better for my needs?

■ How much RAM do I need?

■ If I buy this PC, can I get it with that monitor?

You can find the answers to many questions by reading the spec sheet next to the PC. But remember that such sheets rarely give important information, such as the number and type of open expansion slots and how the RAM's installed. Ask the salesperson for a detailed spec sheet from the manufacturer or for the manufacturer's phone number, so you can fill in the details.

If the store has a service center, talk to one of the technicians. Do buyers commonly return any particular models? Which PC would the technician recommend? Company policy may state that the technician can't answer such questions, but asking's always worth a try.

Don't walk into a PC store on Saturday morning and expect to get any help; on Saturday morning, most stores are packed with shoppers, and salespeople are too busy to provide detailed answers. Go shopping right after the store opens or an hour before it closes during the week. Friday night is usually best.

Collecting Pamphlets and Taking Notes

Never leave a store empty-handed. Grab any available pamphlets and spec sheets for the PCs that interest you. If the spec sheets aren't sitting out somewhere, ask the salesperson for copies. Get a printout of the return policy, warranty, and service agreement so that you can examine it at home.

Always carry a small notebook to write down any details about the PCs you look at. Write down the make and model number of each PC and record any details that the pamphlets or the spec sheets don't mention, such as the number of open PCI slots and drive bays. Record any interesting snippets you learn from talking with the salesperson.

Exiting Gracefully Without Purchasing a PC

Retail stores hate having shoppers play with their PCs and then run out and buy a PC from a mail-order company, but — hey! — them's the breaks. After you're done gathering the information that you need or if you just run out of steam and decide to take a break, leave. Don't let guilt or compassion for the salesperson get in your way. Just walk out the door . . . without a PC.

Some PC dealers can be as pushy as vacuum cleaner salespeople. They try to lure you with the day's special or offer you financing options only if you purchase the PC today. Don't listen to them. As a PC buyer, you have two things going for you: Competition in the PC market is stiff, and prices *always* drop. The PC that you can buy for $1,500 today is likely to cost $1,400 (or less) next month. As you're waiting for the next sale to roll around, you can spend some time reading the fine print in the return policy and warranty.

CHAPTER 7

EVALUATING THE ALL-IMPORTANT TRADE-OFFS

IN THIS CHAPTER

- Trimming the sticker price by going with a slower processor
- Adding options and remaining within budget
- Building a balanced system
- Finding the right printer for the right price
- Getting the software that you need

Shopping for a PC on a budget requires you to make some tough decisions. Say that you have $1,500 to spend. The basic system costs $1,200; then you add a printer for $250 and upgrade to a 21-inch monitor for $150. You're already a hundred bucks over budget, and you still want a bigger hard drive and 32MB more RAM. Can you figure out any way to get everything that you want for $1,500?

Of course not!

You can, however, make some tradeoffs that get you *almost* everything you want within your budget. You may manage to save $100 by going with a slightly slower processor than you wanted. Maybe you can find a 19-inch monitor with a large viewing area that costs less than that 21-inch monitor. If audio quality isn't that important to you, you can cut back on the sound board.

This chapter describes the most important money-saving tradeoffs that you can make without overly compromising the integrity of the PC. Here you learn how to put together a balanced system while staying true to your budget.

Price versus Power

Processor manufacturers are constantly cranking up the speed of their processors. With each passing month, you're likely to see the processor speeds jump by 100 MHz. Typically accompanying that speed jump is a $100 to $200 dip in the price of the previous top-of-the-line system (with a slightly slower processor).

If you're the type of person who simply must have the latest, greatest product on the market, a 100 MHz performance boost may seem important to you. For the rest of us, a 100 MHz boost is imperceptible. In fact, many speedy processors already run beyond the speed that the motherboard's communications network (the system bus) supports. For instance, the system bus may handle communications at a top speed of 133 MHz, whereas the processor runs at 500-600 MHz.

To alleviate the bottleneck between the processor and the system bus, the processor has its own fast memory area (called *cache*, pronounced "cash"). The processor can move data into and out of the cache, so it doesn't need to wait for the system bus. However, at processor speeds of 500-600 MHz, the processor is testing the upper limits of the cache and system bus, and a 100 MHz jump will be barely noticeable.

In short, going with a slower processor is one of the best ways to trim the sticker price. Just make sure that you stay in the same family of processors. You may not notice a performance difference between a 500 MHz and a 400 MHz Pentium III, for example, but you do notice a significant difference between a 500 MHz Pentium III and a 400 MHz Celeron, because the Pentium III has a superior design, includes 512KB cache (as compared to the Celeron's 128KB), and supports a 100 or 133 MHz bus (as compared to Celeron's 66 MHz bus).

Don't Skimp on the RAM

Windows 98 claims that it can run on a PC with as little as 16MB RAM. Sure, it runs, but it's constantly shuffling data back and forth between RAM and the much slower hard disk. With each additional program that you run in Windows, the problem worsens. You launch a program, and it doesn't pop right up on-screen like before. You open a document and twiddle your thumbs waiting for it to actually open. Eventually, your system crashes or informs you that it's exhausted its memory banks.

Besides, RAM is relatively inexpensive — typically $1 to $3 per megabyte. By cutting the amount of RAM in half — say, from 64MB to 32MB — you save less than 60 bucks and significantly compromise the PC's performance. Figure 7-1 shows the RAM options and prices for a typical desktop PC at an online shopping site.

Start with a baseline of 64MB RAM. For lighter use (word processing and e-mail only), cut that in half — to 32MB. For heavier use (games, graphics, page layout, multimedia), double the baseline amount — to 128MB RAM.

Figure 7-1: Skimping on RAM doesn't save you much money.

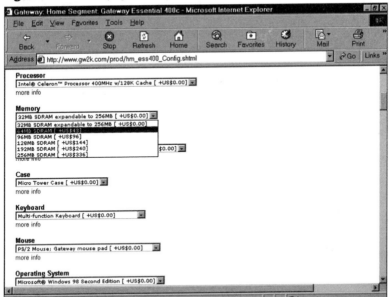

How Much Hard Drive Do You Really Need?

As you scan PC ads, you're likely to come across PCs with anywhere from 4 to 20GB hard drives. Does anybody really need 20GB of hard drive space? I know that I don't. I'd need five years just to pack a 20GB drive *half* full.

Some people, however, need larger hard drives. If you're planning on installing a computer game library or using your PC to edit video clips, you may need a hard drive with more than 10GB. Most PC users find that any hard drive with more than 5GB is sufficient. For the best value, look for a hard drive in the 5 to 8GB range. Don't consider anything less than 4GB.

SCSI (pronounced "skuzzy," for *S*mall *C*omputer *S*ystem *I*nterface) drives are excellent for network servers, but if you're buying a desktop PC, stick with the cheaper EIDE (Enhanced Intelligent Drive Electronics) drive. You don't see much of a performance difference on desktop PCs. (For more information about hard drive options, refer to Chapter 8.)

CD-ROM and DVD Options

Except for some "free" systems, all PCs include a CD-ROM drive as a standard feature. You need a CD-ROM drive for installing most programs, playing games, and using reference materials, such as multimedia encyclopedias. Don't settle for a CD-ROM drive that's slower than 32X, which can play most current CD titles at top speed.

If you're planning on "burning" (recording data on) your own CDs, check into CD-R (Recordable) and CD-RW (ReWritable) drives. A CD-R enables you to record once to the disc; CD-RW enables you to re-record over the same disc.

Not quite a standard feature on new PCs, DVD drives are growing in popularity. Short for *digital versatile disk* or *digital video disk*, DVD discs can store more than seven times as much data as a CD, making them perfect for playing high-tech games and storing full-length movies, interactive presentations, and multimedia reference materials, such as encyclopedias.

I strongly recommend that you consider a system with a DVD drive (which adds about $80 to $100 to the system cost). Although you may never intend to watch movies on your PC, you're sure to be happy that you have a DVD drive after companies start placing huge multimedia reference libraries and clip art collections on DVD. Get a DVD drive that's no slower than 4.8X.

Most DVD drives can handle both DVD and CD-ROM discs, but ask to make sure.

Don't Go Cheap on the Monitor

In shopping for a monitor, keep one important fact in mind: You can't upgrade it. If you're not happy with the monitor six months after you purchase your PC, you must replace the monitor — you can't just plug in more RAM or a new processor.

On the other hand, remain aware that the monitor is one of the most expensive of PC components. If you're looking for a serious place to cut the system cost and you don't mind staring at a dinky screen, you can pick up a 15-inch monitor for cheap. For the sake of your eyes and your future happiness, however, I recommend at least a 17-inch monitor with a resolution of at least 1024-by-768. Resolution is measured by the number of dots that make up the display; the more dots, the crisper the image.

What About the Display Card?

A fancy monitor that you yoke to a crummy display card is going to result in lousy performance. So should you choose the best display card on the market? Not necessarily. If most of your computing chores are of the standard household or business variety (typing, personal finance, Internet), a display card in the $50 to $100 range is fine. Serious gamers and graphic artists want to look for a 3D-graphics accelerator card, which costs anywhere from $150 to $1000.

Look for systems with AGP (Accelerated Graphics Port) rather than PCI (Peripheral Connect Interconnect) graphics. Intel developed the AGP standard especially for 3D video games and other graphics intensive software. I've seen several sub-$1,000 systems that feature AGP graphics cards with 8MB RAM (which is plenty for most uses). The slower PCI graphics cards are on their way out, but if you have only five hundred bucks to spend, PCI isn't bad. Just make sure that you get a card with at least 4MB RAM — and the more the better

Check your hardware requirements list to determine the type of card that you need. Computer games may require a specific make and model.

Audio on a Budget

Unless you plan on watching DVD movies or playing high-tech games on your PC, you don't need the latest, greatest PC audio hardware. Any Wavetable sound card and a set of 5-10 watt stereo speakers suffice. Most sound cards support Wavetable synthesis, which combines digital recording samples from various instruments and combines these samples to generate more realistic playback. Most PC packages now include sound cards with Wavetable support and a decent set of speakers, as shown in Figure 7-2. Don't splurge on the sound system, unless audio quality is one of your main priorities.

Figure 7-2:   A mid-range sound system (with two speakers and a subwoofer) is usually sufficient even for most games. (Photo courtesy of Creative Labs, Inc.)

Shopping for Backup Convenience

Manufacturers, trainers, computer gurus, and even your close friends and relatives are sure to tell you how important backing up the programs and data on your system is. Few of these sources, however, recommend any tools for making the backup operation convenient. You can't realistically back up everything on a 4GB hard drive to 1.44MB floppy disks. If you try, you find that it takes you at least a day, and you end up with a stack of disks that reaches from the floor to the ceiling.

If you're on a tight budget and enjoy living dangerously, forego the backup drive. Otherwise, make sure that your PC includes a backup drive with high-capacity removable storage media. Use Table 7-1 as your guide.

Table 7-1:   Backup Options

Drive Type	*Description*
Tape	Stores data on inexpensive, cassettelike tapes (typically 1-8GB per cassette). Using tape is a slow way to perform backups, but with good backup software and high-capacity tapes, you can schedule backups for whenever you're not using your PC.

(continued)

Table 7-1:   Back-up Options *(continued)*

Drive Type	Description
CD-RW	Stores data on inexpensive RW CDs, each holding more than 600MB. The drive is a little more expensive than a tape drive, but the media (CDs) are cheaper, and the drive works faster.
Zip	Stores data on special Zip disks (100 or 250MB per disk). Although using a Zip drive is better than backing up to floppy disks, you still need to be there to change disks while performing backups. (Many new systems come with Zip drives.)
Jaz	Stores data on 1-2GB cartridges nearly as fast as a hard drive. Jaz drives are great for backups, but they're somewhat costly for both the drive and its cartridges.
LS-120	Imation's SuperDisk drive stores up to 120MB on a single floppylike disk and can handle standard 1.44MB floppy disks as well. It's not bad for bargain-hunters, but 120MB disks lack the storage capacity for heavy-duty backups.

USB (Universal Serial Bus) ports are great for connecting backup drives or other external devices later. You simply plug the device into one of the USB ports just as if you were plugging a phone line into a wall jack. If you decide to put off the purchase of a backup drive, at least make sure that your PC has one or two USB ports.

Modems and Networking Options

Although modem and network card options are plentiful, the available connection services limit your choices. If you're buying a PC to connect to a network, the network's existing hardware dictates the type of network card that you need. Expect to spend about $50. If your phone company doesn't offer DSL (digital subscriber line) service in your area and your cable company doesn't offer digital Internet access, you need a 56 Kbps modem.

Expect to pay $50 to $100 for a good, standard modem. If you're planning on using the modem for business and need fax, voice support, caller ID, distinctive rings, callback security, speakerphone support, and other options, the price can climb to more than $300. Don't pay for something you're not going to use.

Stay away from WinModems or Windows Modems (also known as "controllerless" modems), which use the system's processor rather than the modem's own processor. This isn't bad for the modem, but it places additional work on the system processor and slows down the system.

Don't Forget the Printer

On the surface, selecting a printer looks easy: Do you want a color printer or black-and-white? Laser or inkjet? Printer options (and price ranges), however, are nearly limitless. You find everything from sub-$100 black-and-white printers to all-in-one machines that can print, copy, fax, and scan for more than $600. You may even encounter heavy-duty business printers that cost more than $5,000!

Use Table 7-2 as your guide to the most important features you want to consider in selecting a printer.

Table 7-2: Major Printer Features

Feature	*Criteria*
Laser	Fast but expensive.
Inkjet	High-quality on a budget.
Color	Essential for the occasional greeting card or banner. Make sure that the color and black ink or toner cartridges are separate so that you don't waste the color ink if you run out of black.

(continued)

Table 7-2: Major Printer Features (continued)

Feature	Criteria
Quality	Prints at 600 dpi (dots per inch) or higher. If you need near-photo-quality output, go with 1,200 dpi or higher.
Speed	Prints at 4-8 ppm (pages per minute) or faster for monochrome, 2-4 ppm for color.
Price	Expect to pay $200 for a good inkjet and $300 for an entry-level laser. If you want a combination fax, copier, scanner, inkjet printer, expect to pay more than $600.
Consumables	Expect 3-10 cents per page. If the printer's cheap but the ink cartridges are expensive and print few pages, you pay in the long run.
Envelope Feed	The paper tray needs to feature an easy way to feed business envelopes into the printer.

Warning

Many dealers sweeten a PC package by throwing in a cheap printer and a cheaper scanner that share the printer port and aren't very nice about sharing. If you want to scan and print, you can avoid problems by purchasing an all-in-one printer. You save desk space that way, too.

Getting the Software that You Need

You never want to base PC selection solely on the software selection that comes with the machine, because some dealers use the software to hook unwary shoppers into buying obsolete PCs. A good software bundle, however, can significantly add to the system's value.

Make sure that the software that comes with the PC is software you're going to use. If you use Microsoft Word at work, for example, and the system comes with the Microsoft Works Suite or Microsoft Home Essentials, you're going to be sorely disappointed with the scaled-down version of Microsoft Word that comes in the cheaper suite.

Similarly, if the dealer dangles a home-productivity or kids learning package in front of your nose, don't snap it up until you try the software. I've purchased educational software bundles for my kids thinking that they'd be giddy over the cool programs only to find them playing with some free educational program that they found on the Web.

If you're not going to use it, it's not valuable.

Microsoft and other software companies commonly offer special upgrade deals for the software installed on a new system. For instance, if the PC comes with Works, and you want Microsoft Office, you can upgrade to Office for one-third to half of the cost.

CHAPTER 8
PERSONALIZING YOUR PC PURCHASE

IN THIS CHAPTER

- Building your own PC package
- Upgrading key components at the time of purchase
- Adding a game controller
- Tacking on a scanner or digital camera

As you're checking out ads and pacing the aisles at your local computer store, you can easily get hung up on package deals. Should you buy the Celeron system with the 8GB hard drive and 96MB RAM or the Athlon system with the 4.3GB hard drive and the 64MB RAM? You'd really like that Athlon system, but it comes with only a 15-inch monitor, and you prefer that 17-inch monitor that the Celeron system includes.

Take off the blinders and broaden your scope. Most dealers enable you to "build" your own PC by *upgrading* the package. If you like everything about the PC except the amount of RAM, have the dealer install more RAM. Don't like that dime-store monitor? Upgrade to the big-screen Trinitron. Dissatisfied with the crummy printer? Buy the printer separately.

Of course, any upgrade adds to the PC's price and delivery time, but it also adds to the useful life of your PC, making you less likely to need to upgrade the PC any time soon. This chapter describes some of the most common upgrade options available.

Price versus Power

I'm looking at an ad right now for a desktop PC with a 500 MHz Pentium III processor. You can upgrade to a 550 MHz processor for only $225. *Only* $225?! An additional $225 is *way* too much for an incremental speed boost that you can't even notice.

If you're looking for power and have an extra couple hundred bucks to spend, go with a system that's built around the next generation of processor rather than a slight bump up in speed. Spending extra money to move up from a Celeron-based system to a Pentium III-based system makes sense, because you *do* notice a performance difference between the two systems. Bumping up the processor speed a notch just to be the first person on the block to own a top-of-the-line system is insane.

Ordering Additional RAM

RAM is one of the cheapest and easiest components to upgrade later, and RAM prices always drop. If you're strapped for cash and are sure that the system has enough RAM for your current needs, don't worry about adding RAM now. Just make sure that the system has open RAM sockets so that you can pop in new RAM modules later without removing existing modules.

If you're not a weekend mechanic type and the cost of the extra 32MB RAM is within your budget, get the RAM now. Although adding RAM modules is easy, if you're not comfortable popping the PC's hood, you're going to be happy that you got the extra RAM at the time of purchase.

Read the warranty. Some warranties state that if anyone other than a certified technician or the manufacturer installs the RAM (or any other component), the warranty is void.

Going for a Bigger, Faster Hard Drive

Although you don't want to waste money by buying more hard drive storage than you need, check the cost of upgrading the hard drive. Many dealers offer double the storage capacity for an extra fifty bucks, and you can walk away knowing that you're not going to be strapped for storage space for years down the road.

You should also consider the speed of the drive, and this is the area where things start to become complicated. Except for SCSI hard drives (see the Tip at the end of this section), most desktop PCs come with ATA (AT Attachment) or DMA (Direct Memory Access) hard drives, which conform to any of several ATA standards, as I describe in Table 8-1. Make sure that the system comes with at least an ATA/33 or a DMA/33 drive.

Table 8-1: ATA Hard Drive Speeds

ATA Standard	Maximum Transfer Rate (In Megabytes Per Second)
ATA	8.3MBs
Fast ATA	11.1MBs
ATA-2	16.6MBs
ATA-3	16.6MBs. Some ATA-3 drives support Ultra DMA/33 at a maximum transfer rate of 33MBs.
ATA-4	33MBs with support for Ultra DMA Mode 2, which you use in Ultra DMA/33 drives.
ATA-5	44.4MBs with support for Ultra DMA Mode 4. 66.6MBs with support for Ultra DMA Mode 5. Commonly known as Ultra ATA/66 or Ultra DMA/66 drives.

To further complicate matters, you can install a faster hard drive on a system that doesn't support the faster drive. An unethical manufacturer can install an ATA/66 drive on a system that supports only ATA/33, for example, in which case the $100 bucks that you spent for the faster drive is wasted. Ask if the BIOS chip set (the component set that acts as the soul of the motherboard) supports the hard drive's maximum speed or find out which chip set is installed and contact the chip set manufacturer.

SCSI drives are designed for improved performance on network servers, where several PCs may be requesting data from a single drive at the same time. On a desktop PC, IDE, or EIDE (ATA) drives work just fine and cost much less.

Upgrading the Monitor

Don't get carried away with the monitor. Upgrading to one of those nifty, new LCD flat-panel displays can cost as much as the rest of the PC. A good 15- or 17-inch CRT (Cathode Ray Tube, a standard monitor) is sufficient for most users. Gamesters, graphic artists, and desktop publishing aficionados may opt for a 19- or 21-inch CRT.

Focus more on the display card that's installed. In many cases, you can upgrade from 4 to 8MB of video RAM for less than $50 and make the PC perform much faster.

Remember to look for a system that offers an AGP graphics card.

Accessorizing Your PC

PC merchants know that most shoppers view the PC more as a cool toy than as a useful tool. Sure, first-time buyers *say* that they're going to use the PC to organize their finances and manage their careers, but they really want the PC for playing cool computer games, e-mailing scanned photos to friends, and finding cheap flights to Aruba. To take advantage of the situation, PC dealers pack their ads with cool toys, such as scanners, digital cameras, and game controllers, hoping to snare an impulse-buyer.

Hey, indulging yourself is okay — just don't let your weakness for impulse-spending stick you with a bunch of junky hardware. Many of the toys that dealers offer at the time of purchase are nothing more than warehouse remnants. Before you drop $150 on a digital camera, read the following sections and do some additional research to find out what's currently available.

Adding a game controller

One of the most popular items that people buy when purchasing a new PC — especially a family PC — is a game controller (typically, a joystick). Unwary shoppers often think that one game controller is as good as any other and see a $20 joystick as a bargain. Nothing is further from the truth. Your kid may play with that $20 joystick for less than five minutes before you start hearing him yelling words you didn't even know he knew.

Spend as much time and effort shopping for a game controller as you do in shopping for a monitor. Tell your kid to read reviews in game magazines or ask friends for their recommendations. Take your kid to the store to try out some game controllers on display.

Never buy any extras at the time that you purchase your PC unless you have time to research them, no matter how convenient picking up everything at once seems. It's just too easy to get stuck with shoddy equipment when you're buying a PC.

Adding a scanner

A couple years ago, I bought a cheap scanner: $129 minus a $50 rebate. It even came with an adapter for the parallel port so that it could share the port with my printer. Well, sometimes the printer worked; and sometimes the scanner worked; and every once in awhile, the printer and scanner both worked. That cheap scanner cost me hours of frustrating, time-consuming troubleshooting.

Fortunately, with the introduction of all-in-one printers (which print, scan, copy, and fax) and USB ports, scanner problems may be a thing of the past — but not until scanner manufacturers empty the old scanners from their warehouses. Until then, dealers are going to offer you great deals on scanners that are far from being great deals. Here's my advice:

- Avoid scanners that share the printer port.

- If you think you may need to scan from books or magazines, get a flat-bed scanner, as shown in Figure 8-1. (Sheet-fed scanners roll individual pages through the scanner.)

- To conserve desk space, get an all-in-one printer with scanning capabilities. (Few all-in-one machines have flat-bed scanning, however, so if you need a flat-bed scanner, buy the scanner and printer separately.)

- Get a color scanner that can scan at a resolution of 600dpi (dots per inch) or higher and 36-bit color, to ensure that scanned images will be nearly as good as your color photos.

Most scanners include OCR (optical character recognition) software, which transforms scanned text into text that you can edit in a word processor. Even a good OCR makes mistakes in converting scanned text to editable text (for example, turning 7 into %), but lousy OCR programs are nearly useless. Find out which OCR program comes with the scanner and do some research.

Figure 8-1: You can scan just about anything by using a flat-bed scanner.

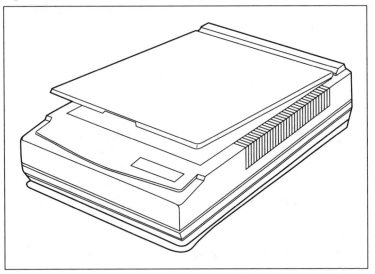

You find plenty of SCSI scanners on the market but few PCs with a SCSI port. If you're purchasing a PC as part of a package, the dealer should make sure that you don't get a scanner you can't use — but check it anyway, just in case he doesn't. A SCSI scanner may come with a special SCSI expansion board that works only with the scanner (not with other SCSI devices).

Buying a digital camera

The best time to buy a digital camera isn't while you're shopping for a PC, although you find plenty of merchants willing to give you a great deal on a digital camera if you purchase it *now*. Digital cameras offer simply too many options and specifications for you to consider, such as maximum colors and resolutions, battery life, storage capacity, options for connecting the camera to your PC, preview screens, and so on.

Research digital cameras thoroughly before you buy one and check them out at a local store. Don't drop $150 on a cheap digital camera before you check out the quality of image it produces. You may find that you get better pictures with one of those disposable box cameras. If you need the photos digitized, most photo developers can do that for you and place the pictures on a CD, or you can use your scanner. You don't get the immediate gratification that a digital camera offers, but you save a wad of cash and enjoy better results.

Surge suppressors and continuous-power supplies

To prevent turning your new $1,000 PC into a piece of burnt toast, purchase a good surge suppressor or UPS (uninterruptible power supply). A surge suppressor prevents high voltage current (from lightning or power surges) from reaching your equipment. A UPS uses a battery to provide a continuous flow of current to the PC during power outages and fluctuations.

Which is better? A UPS, because it protects equipment against lightning damage and long-term damage from power fluctuations and prevents your PC from shutting down during a power outage, so you won't lose documents you haven't yet saved to your hard disk. If you're looking for a cheap way to protect your equipment against lightning damage and aren't worried about data loss from power outages, a $25 surge suppressor is sufficient. Expect to pay over $100 for a basic UPS.

Table 8-2 lists the qualities that you want to look for in a good surge suppressor. Table 8-3 shows you what to look for in a good UPS.

Table 8-2: Important Surge Suppressor Features

Feature	Description
UL rating	400 or less. The UL rating represents the maximum voltage that the surge suppressor lets pass through it.
Energy Absorption Rating	400 or more. The energy-absorption rating represents the amount of energy that the suppressor can absorb before it's toast.
Outlets	6 power outlets, 1 modem outlet, 1 phone line outlet. Make sure that you can plug all your equipment, including the modem, into the surge suppressor.
Guarantee	Money-back plus replacement cost for any equipment that a power surge damages.

Tip

Some surge suppressors and UPS's have power outlets that are placed too close together, making it impossible to plug in two devices in adjacent outlets. Make sure the plugs are spaced far enough apart.

Table 8-3: Important UPS Features

Feature	Description
Volt-ampere output	200-300VA. Most Pentium systems require a UPS with a rating of 300VA to keep the power supply running. If you plug in additional devices, you need a UPS with a higher VA rating. Multiply the amperage of each device by the voltage (usually 120V) and add the results. (You can usually find the amperage and voltage for a device at the back of its owner's manual.)
Reliability	Online or Ferroresonant, which provide a steady flow of power in switching from direct to battery power. Avoid standby or offline UPSes, which experience a slight dip in power in switching from direct to battery power.

Feature	Description
Outlets	2 continuous-power outlets; 4 surge-suppressor outlets; 1 modem outlet; 1 phone line outlet.
Battery replacement	User replaceable. Check the price of replacement batteries and whether the unit uses a single battery or multiple batteries.
Indicator lights	Display that shows whether the unit is using direct power or battery power, whether the batteries are running low and if you need to replace them, and whether the power outlet is correctly wired.
System shutdown	Automatic system shutdown if the duration of the power outage exceeds the available time that the batteries can supply power.
Guarantee	Money-back plus replacement cost for any equipment that a power surge damages.

Upgrading the Warranty and Service

I'm not one to recommend service agreements for refrigerators and TV sets, but for PCs, I think that they're a good idea. Your PC should run trouble-free for at least three years, but if something goes wrong before then, you're going to need help.

On the surface, a three-year warranty is better than a one-year warranty, but a good one-year warranty is better than a bad three-year warranty. Some warranties cover only some parts, and you pay for the service; others cover all parts and service and may even provide on-site service so that you don't need to lug the PC into the service center or ship it to the manufacturer. Read the warranty and service agreement carefully.

Most dealers offer premium service agreements (many with on-site service) at the time of the sale for an additional cost. Unless you have a friend or relative who's a PC guru, I recommend that you get on-site service for at least the first year that you own your PC.

Building a PC Package on the Web

Although most retailers can figure out some way to get you the PC and accessories that you want, trying to build your own PC at a retail store is stressful. You're less likely to experiment with various options if you can see a line of angry shoppers waiting to talk with the salesperson.

The best place to build your own package is on the Web. Most mail-order PC dealers have Web sites where you can select from available options and see immediately how each upgrade (or downgrade) affects the price. To configure your own PC package at Gateway, for example, take the following steps:

1. Connect to the Internet and run a Web browser (or get a friend to do it).

2. In your browser's Address text box, type www.gw2k.com and press Enter. This opens Gateway's home page, which has links for desktop PCs, portable PCs, and PC add-ons.

3. Click the link for <u>desktops</u>. This opens Gateway's Desktops page, which displays links for different desktop PC models.

4. Click the <u>want one?</u> link for the line of PCs with which you want to start.

5. Click the option for the processor type and basic software that you want and then click the Next button. The site shows you the components that come in the standard package and the price of the system.

6. Click the Customize It button. The site displays a form that you can use to choose options.

7. Scroll down the form and choose the desired components, as shown in Figure 8-2.

8. After you reach the bottom of the form, click the Update Price button. The site recalculates and displays the price.

Figure 8-2: Build a custom PC package online at Gateway's Web site.

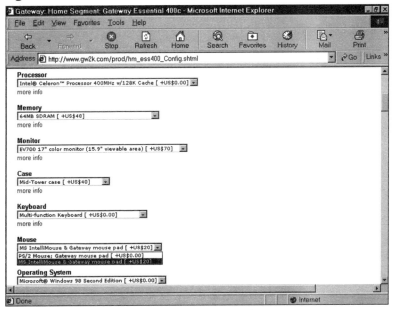

If you have a credit card that's not maxed out, you can even purchase your custom PC right on the Web. Before you do, check out the offerings at some other sites, such as Dell (at www.dell.com), Compaq (at www.compaq.com), and MicronPC (at www.micronpc.com).

Before you order, read the fine print, check the warranty and service agreement, and figure in the shipping costs.

CHAPTER 9

FINANCING YOUR PC PURCHASE

IN THIS CHAPTER

- Saving money by paying up front
- Calculating the cost of finance options
- The importance of paying by credit card
- Evaluating leasing options

Congratulations — you've found the PC of your dreams. Not only can it run all the software on your list, but it's also built for the future and has plenty of room for upgrades later. It even matches the sofa in your den.

Now, how are you going to pay for it? Should you pay cash? Write a check? Stick it on your credit card? Finance it through the dealer? Take out a home improvement loan? How about leasing it for a couple of years and picking up a better PC down the road?

All these financing options are available, but few are smart. As you learn in this chapter, paying cash or writing a check is never a good idea, and if you ever sat down with a calculator and your mortgage statement, you know that refinancing for a larger amount is rarely worth it. To avoid getting caught in a financing fiasco, use this chapter as your guide.

Paying Cash

Obviously, you can avoid finance charges by paying for the PC in full at the time that you purchase it. But even if you have the cash gathering dust in your bank account, paying by cash, check, money order, or debit card is never a good idea. Doing so simply makes you a more vulnerable consumer.

If you pay with cash or the equivalent, the merchant gets what the merchant wants from the transaction — your money. But do you get what you want? If the merchant fails to deliver your PC in good condition or the PC stops working in two weeks, the merchant has little incentive to correct the problem. By using your credit card, you can enlist the help of the credit card company or the Federal Trade Commission if things go wrong.

If you have the cash, pay with a credit card that levies no finance charges for 30 days after the charge and then pay off your balance in full.

Knowing Your Credit Card Rights

The Fair Credit Billing Act (FCBA) of 1975 gives you a great deal of leverage in dealing with unfair credit card billing practices and merchants who fail to deliver their products. You don't need to read the FCBA in full, but you should know the following:

■ If the dealer fails to deliver the merchandise according to your agreement, contact the merchant and *immediately* send a letter to your credit card company. Yelling at a customer service representative may make you feel better, but it gives you no protection under the FCBA.

■ The credit card company must receive your letter of complaint within 60 days from the time you receive the statement showing the charge, so don't procrastinate.

■ The FCBA doesn't protect you against shoddy products. In some states, however, you can withhold payment from the credit card company for unsatisfactory merchandise just as you can withhold payments from a merchant. Doing so usually gets the credit card company on your side. Contact your state's Better Business Bureau or Attorney General's Office to learn about your consumer rights. (Many credit card companies print your rights on the back of your statement.)

State laws typically apply only to purchases made from merchants in the same state and pretty close to where you live (within 100 miles of your billing address). Check your state law.

If your letter of complaint to your credit card company fails to bring the desired results, call the local branch of the Federal Trade Commission. If your credit card company is national, address the issue to the FTC's main office: Correspondence Branch, Federal Trade Commission, Washington, D.C. 20580. You can check out your consumer rights online at the Federal Trade Commission's Web site at www.ftc.gov (see Figure 9-1).

To help others avoid the same problems you encountered, file a complaint with the Better Business Bureau. Although the Better Business Bureau can't force the merchant to stand behind its products and services, it can make your complaint public. In addition, if you mention your intent to a file a complaint to the merchant, the merchant may be more willing to cooperate.

Figure 9-1:   The Federal Trade Commission's Web site.

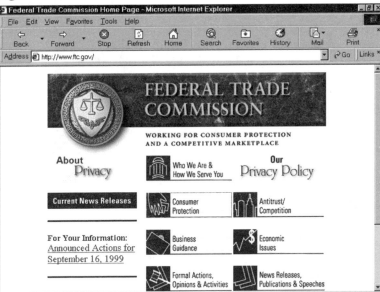

For a list of low-rate credit cards (for a small fee), call RAM Research Corp at 1-800-344-7714.

Financing Your PC through the Merchant

Most dealers are happy to finance your PC for you. Unfortunately, the dealer typically charges you the same percentage or higher than you pay by using your credit card. In addition, the FCBA doesn't provide you with any protection if you finance through the dealer. The FCBA provides protection only for *open-end* credit accounts, accounts that allow you to add charges to your account over time. Dealers typically offer finance options in the form of *close-end* accounts, in which you borrow a set amount of money and then pay it off according to a fixed schedule.

Many dealers use the 60-months-same-as-cash pitch to get you to walk out of the store with a PC. I love these deals, especially if my cash isn't flowing as smoothly as usual. I can get what I want, when I want it, and then pay it off two months down the road. This approach, however, can be very risky. Almost all same-as-cash deals accrue interest over the two months during which you have possession of the merchandise before making a payment. If you fail to pay in full by the specified date, you must pay all that back interest. And, because the FCBA provides no protection for dealer-financed agreements, you can't go crying to the Federal Trade Commission if the dealer fails to deliver the PC on time or in good condition.

Calculating Finance Charges

If you have a mortgage, you know that finance charges can add up to much more than the cost of the house itself. Fortunately, you rarely pay more in finances than the cost of the PC, but finance charges can add significantly to the full cost of the PC. During the writing of this book, for example, a major PC dealer was offering to finance PCs at 14.9 percent for a three-year loan. For a $1,500 PC, you end up paying $1,869. In other words, you end up paying nearly 25 percent more for the PC.

You don't need to be an accountant to determine your total finance charges. Simply take the following steps:

1. Multiply your monthly payment by the total number of months you're paying to determine the total cost of the PC plus finance charges.

2. Subtract the cost of the PC. What's left are the finance charges.

If, after all my warnings, you decide to finance your PC through the dealer, compare finance charges from various dealers before you sign any agreements.

Go to Your Bank

I've ruled out paying by cash or check or by financing through the merchant. The credit card option is okay . . . assuming that you have the money to pay your balance after the bill arrives. So where does that leave you? At the bank.

If you just don't have the money at the time that your credit card bill arrives, check the loan rates at your bank or credit union. If you're lucky (very lucky), your bank may loan you the money to pay off your credit card balance at a slightly lower rate than you can get from the merchant or your credit card company.

Ask your banker if you qualify for any special loans, such as education or small-business loans at lower rates.

Leasing Options

Leasing a PC looks good on the surface. You get a brand new PC right now for a low, low monthly fee. At the end of the lease, you return the PC and lease a new one. Few users who lease PCs, however, have the foresight to realize that, over the term of the lease, they're going to be configuring, installing programs on, and saving documents to the loaner PC. How are you going to get all that stuff from the old PC to the new one? Transferring documents isn't that difficult, but successfully transferring programs and configuration settings is nearly impossible.

In addition to that little problem, leasing a PC costs more than buying a PC outright. Right now, I'm looking at a 24-month leasing option for $108/month on a $2,199 PC. Bottom line — you pay $2,592 total . . . and you must give back the PC after the 24 months are up! Even if you flunked fifth-grade math, you can see that this lease deal is no bargain.

On trade-in agreements, the dealer typically gets to decide which PC you get as a replacement at the end of the term. Read the fine print and look for phrases such as "company's sole discretion" and "terms subject to change without notice."

Return Policies and Restocking Fees

The UPS driver finally arrives with your PC. You anxiously tear into the boxes to unveil your new toy. After you finally dig through the packing material, you see that the packing box is built better than the PC. You call the merchant to complain, and he tells you in an overly patient voice that you can simply return the machine . . . you just must pay a 15 percent restocking fee and all shipping costs.

Can merchants do this sort of thing? Yes. *Do* they do it? Yes. I once fell victim to the restocking-fee scam after the guy at the neighborhood auto parts store sold me the wrong catalytic converter. He was determined to withhold 20 percent of the refund for "restocking fees" and only rescinded after I started howling and foaming at the mouth. Figure 9-2 shows a return clause from a respectable mail-order merchant that would make any consumer cringe. (Names are changed to protect the guilty.)

Figure 9-2:   Read the return policy for warning signs.

> Shoddy PCs Return Policy
>
> ShoddyPCs will refund the original purchase price of the Product and Accessories. Shipping, handling, and any insurance fees (including applicable sales taxes) that you paid when you purchased your product and accessories are not refundable and will be deducted from your refund.

Fortunately, most reliable merchants don't charge a restocking fee, but you don't know until you ask. Read the fine print and examine the return policy closely *before* you purchase a PC.

Make sure, too, that you can return the PC within 30 to 60 days of the purchase (the longer the better). Because some consumers take unfair advantage of extended return policies (to "borrow" PCs and then return them), most merchants offer only limited return periods.

After unpacking your PC and accessories, save the boxes. Most merchants accept returns only if you send them back in the original packaging.

Following Up on Price Guarantees

If you purchase a PC from a dealer who guarantees the lowest prices, follow up on that guarantee. With some dealers, if you find a better price on the same PC within a specified number of days from the time that you purchase your PC (typically two weeks), the dealer refunds the price difference plus a certain percentage of the difference.

Keep flipping through the PC ads after you purchase your PC to see whether you can cash in on the guarantee.

Trimming the Cost by Taking a Tax Deduction

If you plan on using your PC for business purposes, don't overlook the fact that your PC can save you money on your taxes. If you normally pay 28 percent in taxes, for example, and you buy a $2,000 PC for your business, you don't need to pay taxes on that $2,000, so you save $560. Of course, you're not *making* any money by buying the PC, but figuring in the tax deduction, that $2,000 PC ends up costing you only $1,440.

Can you claim your PC as a tax deduction? That depends on whether you use the PC to make money. If you're just blasting away at the evil warships, your PC isn't deductible. Of course, the IRS hangs all sorts of restrictions on the deduction, as the following list describes:

■ If you run a business out of your home and you use the PC 100 percent for business use, you can deduct the cost of the PC and all software.

- You must depreciate the PC over five years (and depreciate software over three years), so you can deduct only one-fifth of the cost each year. (Or you can claim the PC as a Section 179 business expense, essentially fully depreciating the PC the first year you own it.)

- If you use the PC for business *and* pleasure, you can deduct only the percentage that you use for business. (Business use of the PC must exceed 50 percent or you can't claim it as a Section 179 business expense.)

- If you're an employee of a company, you can claim the cost of your PC as an employee expense only if your employer *requires* you to have a PC at home for the company's convenience and productivity. (Employee business expenses start to count only after they exceed two percent of your adjusted gross income.)

Before you claim your PC as a tax deduction, read the rules or consult a qualified tax preparer or CPA (certified public accountant).

Interest on a home-equity loan is deductible, even if the PC is for personal use. The loan reduces the equity in your home, however, and if you can't pay off the loan, you could lose your home. In addition, loan origination fees may wipe out the amount you save in taxes. Read the loan agreement carefully before taking out a home-equity loan.

CLIFFSNOTES REVIEW

Use this CliffsNotes Review to practice what you learn in this book and to build your confidence in finding the best PC at the best price. After you work through the review questions, the problem-solving exercises, and the fun and useful practice projects, you're well on your way to achieving your goal of buying the right PC for your needs.

Q&A

1. To purchase a PC that meets your needs, you should . . .

    a. Buy the best PC on the market.

    b. Read hardware requirements on the sofeware packages.

    c. Test-drive PCs at your local computer store.

2. To ensure that you can upgrade your PC in the future, make sure that . . .

    a. The Pc has open RAM sockets.

    b. The PC has open expansion slots.

    c. The PC has open drive bays.

    d. All the above.

3. Which is better — a PC with a Pentium III 600 MHz or an Athlon 650 MHz processor?

    a. The Pentium 600 MHz PC.

    b. The Athlon 650 MHz PC.

    c. Not enough information to make a judgment.

4. The best way to judge the quality of a monitor's display is to . . .

   a. Choose a monitor with a low dot pitch.

   b. Read magazine reviews from impartial judges.

   c. Pick the monitor with the largest viewable area.

   d. Go to store and check them out.

5. Why is charging a PC on your credit card better than financing through the merchant?

_____

Answers: (1) b. (2) d. (3) c. (4) d. (5) Because the Fair Credit Billing Act provides protection for consumers who purchase products via credit cards.

Scenarios

1. You saw an ad for a PC that looks pretty good. Your next step is to

_____.

2. Your friend just purchased a new PC and wants to give you her old 486. You should

_____.

3. Two dealers are offering comparable PCs at the same price, and you can't decide which one to buy from. You should

_____.

4. For the same price, you can upgrade the RAM from 32MB to 64MB or double the hard drive storage from eight to 16GB. You should _____.

5. You found a great deal for a free PC. You should

_____.

Answers: (1) Make sure that it meets the hardware requirements for the software you want to run. (2) Say, "No thanks," and buy a new PC. (3) Compare the warranties, support, service, and return policies that both dealers offer. (4) Upgrade the RAM to boost the system performance. (5) Read the fine print.

Consider This

■ Did you know that the information you find on software boxes is essential for helping you purchase a PC? Learn how to read a hardware requirements list in Chapter 1, "Assessing Your Computing Needs."

■ Did you know that some of the most important information that you need to make a good PC choice rarely appears in a PC ad? Find out what's missing in most ads in Chapter 4, "Tracking Down the Best Deal."

■ Do you know how to spot an obvious dealer scam and avoid falling for one? Learn about the warning signs in Chapter 5, "Doing Your Homework."

■ Did you know that a balanced PC with a 400 MHz Pentium III processor may run as fast as a poorly designed PC with a 500 MHz Pentium III processor? Learn more in Chapter 7, "Evaluating the All-Important Tradeoffs."

■ Did you know that you can configure your own PC package on the Web? Check out www.gw2k.com, www.dell.com, www.micronpc.com, and www.compaq.com for samples. Learn more in Chapter 8, "Personalizing Your PC Purchase."

Practice Projects

1. Go to a store that sells PC software and write down the hardware requirements from any five software packages in different categories (for example, Productivity, Games, Internet, Graphics, and Desktop Publishing). See Chapter 1 for more information.

2. Find two ads for comparable PCs and list the differences between the PCs. See Chapter 4 for more information.

3. Pick up a popular PC magazine, such as *PC Computing* or *FamilyPC*, and read reviews for three different PCs. Highlight the important features that each discusses. See Chapter 5 for more information.

4. Visit a local PC dealer and look at five different monitors. Do you notice a difference in display size? Clarity? Speed? Glare? Where are the adjustment knobs located? See Chapter 6 for more information.

5. Pick up a financing agreement from your local PC dealer and highlight the phrases and clauses that should concern you. See Chapter 9 for more information.

CLIFFSNOTES RESOURCE CENTER

In shopping for your first PC (or even your second), knowledge is power. The more information that you have at your fingertips about the latest PC technology, specifications, and reviews, the more savvy a shopper you are. CliffsNotes Resource Center shows you the best of the best — links to the best information and advice in print and online about how to select the ideal PC for your needs and budget. But don't think that this Resource Center is all that we have for you; we put all kinds of pertinent information at www.cliffsnotes.com. Look for all the terrific resources at your favorite bookstore or local library and on the Internet. Whenever you're online, make your first stop at www.cliffsnotes.com, where you can find more incredibly useful information about buying a PC.

Books

This CliffsNotes book is one of many great books about buying and using a PC that IDG Books Worldwide, Inc, publishes. So if you want some great books to continue your exploration of the world of PCs, check out some of these IDG Books Worldwide publications, as well as some titles by other publishers:

Buying a Computer For Dummies, by Dan Gookin, takes you a step farther on your quest for the perfect PC. Learn more about deciphering PC ads, sizing up processors and hard drives, and setting up your PC after the purchase. IDG Books Worldwide, Inc.; $19.99 (U.S.).

PCs For Dummies, by Dan Gookin, shows you how to set up and use your PC after it arrives. In this book, Dan translates common computer jargon, goes behind the scenes with the major PC components, and takes you on a tour of the software you need to do something useful (or at least fun). IDG Books Worldwide, Inc.; $19.99 (U.S.).

The Complete Idiot's Guide to PCs, by Joe Kraynak, side-steps the hardware issues to focus on the software that you use to work or play. Joe shows you how to master Windows 98, create, format, and print documents; copy and move files; create your own folders; and optimize your PC. Macmillan Computer Publishing; $16.99 (U.S.).

Windows 98 for Dummies, by Andy Rathbone, explains the most essential software that comes with your new PC (Windows 98). Andy shows you how to master your PC by using Windows 98 to run programs, manage folders and files, enter commands, and even personalize and optimize your PC. IDG Books Worldwide, Inc.; $19.99 (U.S.).

Finding books that IDG Books Worldwide, Inc., publishes is easy. You find them in your favorite bookstores (on the Internet and at a store near you). IDG Books also maintains the following three Web sites that you can use to read about all the books we publish:

- www.cliffsnotes.com
- www.dummies.com
- www.idgbooks.com

Internet

Check out the following Web sites for PC buyer's guides, PC mail-order merchants, consumer protection, shopping advice, and more:

IDG.net, at www.idg.net/, is a great source for product reviews of desktop and notebook PCs and software. This site may be a little high-end for the novice user, but the reviews are very honest, detailed, and useful. After you arrive at the home page, click the Product Reviews and News tab.

ComputerShopper.com, at www.zdnet.com/computershopper/edit/howtobuy, provides details on the latest PC technology on the market and advice on how to evaluate desktop and notebook PCs, monitors, hard drives, CD-ROM and DVD drives, display cards, and much more.

ZDNet, at www.zdnet.com/, is one of the best places on the Web to find PC reviews, ads, and help. This site is the home of the most popular PC magazines, including *PC Computing*, *PC Magazine*, *Family PC*, and *Computer Shopper*. You find plenty of advice and buyer's guides here.

CNET.com, at home.cnet.com/, is an excellent resource for finding information about the latest PC technology and honest reviews of products that just hit the market.

Intel, at www.intel.com, is a little slanted toward Intel-processor-based systems, but Intel's *PC Buyer's Guide* does provide some good information and advice for purchasing a new PC. (You need to poke around a little to find the buyer's guide; try clicking the link for Where to Buy .)

Next time that you're on the Internet, don't forget to drop by www.cliffsnotes.com. We created an online Resource Center that you can use today, tomorrow, and beyond.

Magazines & Other Media

Check out the following magazines for PC and software reviews and rankings and for information on how to use your PC more productively after you get it:

Computer Shopper is a bible for mail-order PC shoppers. This tome contains reviews and advice for purchasing PCs and components along with gobs of ads for manufacturers and mail-order merchants. (Check it out on the Web at www.zdnet.com/computershopper/.)

Family PC is a great magazine for home users, providing excellent information about games, reference tools, educational software, and (of course) PCs designed for the home. (Check it out on the Web at www.zdnet.com/familypc/.)

PC World is a great magazine for reviews of the top PCs on the market, including family, business, and budget PCs. You can find lists of the top 20 to 100 PCs in each category by visiting PC World on the Web. (You can check out the online version of PC World at www.pcworld.com

Consumer Reports ranks popular PCs and provides advice on how to successfully evaluate a PC's quality, power, and reliability. However, not all issues of *Consumer Reports* contain information about PCs. (You can subscribe to the online version of Consumer Reports at *www.consumerreports.org*.)

You can pick up most of these magazines at your local bookstore or newsstand. They're full of ads for the latest PCs, along with reviews and advice on how to pick the PC and software that you need to make your computing experience more fun and productive.

Send Us Your Favorite Tips

In your quest for the perfect PC, have you come across some fantastic deals or information that can help a fellow first-time PC buyer avoid making a poor choice? Perhaps you now realize that getting an ergonomic keyboard was a big mistake. Or you heard about a defect in the latest, greatest processor that all PC shoppers should know about. If you discover a useful tip that helps you become a more savvy PC shopper and you want to share it, the CliffsNotes staff would love to hear from you. Go to our Web site at www.cliffs-notes.com and click the Talk to Us button. If we select your tip, we may publish it as part of *CliffsNotes Daily*, our exciting, free e-mail newsletter. To find out more or to subscribe to a newsletter, go directly to on the Web.

INDEX

CliffsNotes™

Your shortcut to
success™
for over 40 years

Computers and Software
Confused by computers? Struggling with software? Let *CliffsNotes* get you up to speed on the fundamentals — quickly and easily. Titles include:

Balancing Your Checkbook with Quicken®
Buying Your First PC
Creating a Dynamite PowerPoint® 2000 Presentation
Making Windows® 98 Work for You
Setting up a Windows® 98 Home Network
Upgrading and Repairing Your PC
Using Your First PC
Using Your First iMac™
Writing Your First Computer Program

The Internet
Intrigued by the Internet? Puzzled about life online? Let *CliffsNotes* show you how to get started with e-mail, Web surfing, and more. Titles include:

Buying and Selling on eBay®
Creating Web Pages with HTML
Creating Your First Web Page
Exploring the Internet with Yahoo!®
Finding a Job on the Web
Getting on the Internet
Going Online with AOL®
Shopping Online Safely